THE SOCIAL RECORD
OF CHRISTIANITY

BY

JOSEPH McCABE,

Author of
" The Riddle of the Universe To-day," etc.

Published 2000
The Book Tree
Escondido, CA

First Published by Watts & Co.
London, England, 1935

The Social Record of Christianity
ISBN 1-58509-215-0

©2000
THE BOOK TREE
All Rights Reserved

INTRODUCTION

Almost all books on Christianity approach the subject from a theological perspective, but here we find a record of how Christianity has controlled society and the way it functions. Western civilization has been dependent upon the Christian religion for its ethical and moral teachings and, ultimately, its conduct for many centuries.

McCabe demonstrates, however, that the moral and ethical conduct of western civilization has never been that good and that the chief cause of this has been Christianity itself. Once Christianity became fully organized in around the fourth century, the world was almost immediately thrust into a thousand-year period known as "The Dark Ages." This is no probably coincidence.

The Roman Catholic Church, in its confusion and lust for power, has done more to retard human knowledge on this earth than any other institution. This is not a statement aimed at attacking the Church—it is the simple truth. Ernest Renan was conservative in saying, "The triumph of Christianity was the destruction of civil life for a thousand years." General scholarship estimates that book burnings and repression of knowledge by the Church has set us back approximately 2000 years, intellectually. For example, in the sixth century BCE Pythagoras put forth the idea that the earth rotated around the sun. Around 270 BCE a Greek astronomer named Aristarchus went further and proved the sun was a gigantic body and that the Earth revolved around it. He did so with an ingenious method of timing the half-moons. This was accepted knowledge for a few centuries, until the Church came along. Without the turmoil of the Dark Ages and its resulting repression, this idea could have grown and flourished. Instead, we lost this knowledge almost completely and it did not resurface until the 16th century (about 2000 years later) through Copernicus, who was persecuted by the Church for reintroducing it.

In the 3rd century BCE the accurate circumference of the Earth had been determined and measured by Eratosthenes, who was the librarian at Alexandria. But the library was burned in 389 CE and in the eighth century a bishop named Virgilius tried to reintroduce and promote the idea that the earth was round. He was forced to recant. When Christopher Columbus sailed to America, he was without this scientific knowledge. He did not know for certain that the earth was round, and many sailors of the day feared it was flat and that they might fall off the ends of the earth. Discoveries of new lands were immensely delayed since getting an accurate bearing was a problem. We were missing this knowledge for about 1800 years.

Hipparchus had invented longitude and latitude by the 2nd century BCE, but it was never fully used by seafarers until the 1700's. In 1714 the Parliament of England offered a huge reward for solving the problem of determining longitude and it took 50 years, until 1764, before someone succeeded. All told, it took about 1900 years before we came back to the answer. Many such answers were suppressed and lost in the Dark Ages, or had been previously burned by Church authorities. From the fourth century, when Christianity took real power, to the sixth century, Christianity held Grecian philosophy in vassalage—in other words, they allowed it to survive in exchange for its subservience. In the sixth century an Imperial Mandate finally came down and the last schools of Greek philosophy were shut down. In Greek, the word philosophy means "the love of Sophia" or "the love of wisdom." It's been estimated (by George Fox, in *The Vanishing Gods*) that if it wasn't for Christianity combined with a few other Dark Ages problems like plagues and barbaric invasions, we could have gone from Eratosthenes to Einstein in eight or nine centuries instead of twenty-three.

Throughout history, the Church has put up a bitter and persistent opposition to astronomy, geology, biology, paleontology, and evolution. At various times she has also banned or prevented the investigation or practice of medicine, surgery, anesthetics, life insurance, agriculture, the census, printing, gravitation, a round Earth, the heliocentric system, geography in general, and the use of steam and electricity. We know that in 1633 Galileo was forced to recant under the threat of death after he discovered and could scientifically prove that the earth revolved around the sun. This proof was suppressed for years because the Church believed that the earth was the center of the universe and refused to admit otherwise. It is good to have spiritual leadership, but that leadership should not be forced upon people under threats of death and torture, and should be based on truth.

When this "Dark Age" period finally came to a close, we experienced the Renaissance (from the 14th to the 17th centuries). This Renaissance was a rebirth, or revival, of art, literature, and learning, with the major catalyst being Martin Luther's rebellious breakaway from the Church in 1524. The Renaissance could not get started until the old ways of suppression were shaken. That has happened, but only to a certain degree. To this day we still hang on to this socially repressive system, according to McCabe, because it continues to function as an "authority." One of the stumbling blocks, which took so long for us to overcome, was Christianity's acceptance and promotion of slavery throughout the centuries. Even though we no longer practice slavery, hanging on to it for so long set us back greatly in the overall scheme of things.

Christianity has provided this kind of social history, often to dramatic and suppressive extremes. This is based on well-documented, historical fact and is what McCabe has so aptly outlined in this book.

We have added McCabe's other work, *The Lies and Fallacies of the Encyclopedia Britannica*, to this book because it is not only very popular, but serves as a continuation of the main theme. It documents a clear effort by clerical forces to cover up the historical facts surrounding Christianity. McCabe shows exactly how and why vital facts were either changed or removed from the encyclopedia to cast Christianity into a better social and religious light.

Paul Tice

PREFACE

In the year 1871 the statesmen of Japan sent a large delegation to Europe and America to study the moral and social influence of Christianity. Convinced that it was no longer possible or expedient to keep their country a still and stately old-world garden into which no echo of the new age should penetrate, they had decided to blend all that was beautiful in its culture with the strong progressive forces of Western civilization. Missionaries claimed that the Christian religion was one of the most beneficently constructive of these forces, and a body of learned and ideally impartial Japanese were sent to examine the justice of the claim. All were Agnostics and were fully prepared to recommend, for the instruction of the uneducated mass of the people, a religion which would evidently help them to disarm the prejudice of the white nations. But the delegates returned to Japan to report that Christianity " had proved itself less efficacious as an ethical influence in the West than Buddhism had done in the East."

This was not the kind of news that wins banner-headlines in the Press, and the few who heard it were astonished. In 1871 it was still regarded as the first law of European history that Christianity had created Western civilization and was one of the chief causes of the supremacy of the white race. Preachers still assured their congregations how their Church had, eighteen centuries earlier, penetrated the gloom and murk of the ancient world, and the fetters had fallen from the slave, woman was lifted from the dust, the child was taken into loving arms, schools and hospitals began to appear, the blood of gladiators no longer clotted on the sands of the arena . . . The fairy tale is still sufficiently familiar.

The new history, it is true, had already begun to remove the drapery of the myth. Even Gibbon had said that " the banners of the Church had never been seen on the side of the people." Finlay had caustically remarked that if our modern civilization was the outcome of Christianity the length of time between the appearance of the cause and the effect had no parallel in history. Buckle was scornful, and even Lecky, after long chapters of prudent compliments to the new religion, had blandly concluded :

> Few men who are not either priests or monks would not have preferred to live in the best days of the Athenian or the Roman Republics, in the age of Augustus or in the age of the Antonines, rather than in any period that elapsed between the triumph of Christianity and the fourteenth century.

So all the beautiful ideas and influences which Lecky discovers in the new religion were somehow followed by a thousand years—from the fourth to the fourteenth century—in which few men would care to live. It was, he says later, " one of the most contemptible periods in history."

It is no longer possible for one historian to cover so satisfactorily the entire period of the Christian Era that he can give a positive answer to the question whether Christianity helped or hindered the progress of civilization. But the distribution of the field between a hundred specialist workers has led to scientific precision in the establishment of facts, and here I give a summary of the generally accepted results in each section and unite them in a continuous story. In some sense this little work is a re-write of *The Church and the People*, which I published in 1919. But the canvas is broader, and the detail is enriched by fifteen further years of study of social history; though the account of changes in the condition of the workers, who were until recent times four-fifths of the people, remains the chief theme of the work.

J. M.

JOSEPH McCABE

CONTENTS

THE SOCIAL RECORD OF CHRISTIANITY

CHAPTER I

MYTHS ABOUT THE PRIMITIVE CHURCH

THE first correction of the ancient legend which modern history makes is the discovery that Christianity came, not into a world of darkness and the shadow of death, but into a world that had renewed its youth, into the most enlightened, most progressive, most idealistic age that the race had yet known. Imperialism had wrecked the older kingdoms, but it had inaugurated a cosmopolitan life which brought the ideas and ideals of a dozen nations into stimulating contact. The Mediterranean Sea was the heart of the new world ; the ship, rising sometimes to four or five thousand tons and having baths, libraries, and lounges, was its symbol. In fifty coast-cities from Alexandria to Spain the old arts, religions, and polities mingled, and out of the ferment issued in time a new and nobler art, a new civic sense, a new method of attaining knowledge by the direct study of nature and man, and a score or two of new religions, philosophies, and moralities. The stretch of time from 600 B.C. to A.D. 400 was one of the three great progressive

millennia of history.   In the second and maturer half
of that millennium Christianity appeared.

Even the thoughtful but inexpert public commonly
imagine that this advance of the race toward real
civilization relaxed, if it did not cease, when the
Golden Age of Athenian life ended, and that therefore the beginning of the Christian Era marks a period
of decay.   This is entirely wrong.   Art, it is true, lost
the inspiration of genius, but in compensation the love
of beauty spread broadly over the Greco-Roman
world, and the central parts of a hundred cities
gleamed with a marble splendour of which we still find
noble fragments even on the ragged hills of Asia Minor
and in the deserts of Syria and North Africa.   It is
true that no new Plato or Aristotle arose, but instead
there came moralists whose ideals were much nearer
to ours, and they had over the entire Greco-Roman
world an influence immeasurably greater than Plato
and Aristotle had had at Athens ; while those discoveries of the Greek intellect which we now most
appreciate, the principles of science, were carried to
the point at which they begin to disclose their in-
estimable value to the race.   Alexandria under the
Ptolemies and the Romans did more for the world's
intellectual advance than Athens had ever done.

But we are here chiefly concerned with those discoveries which yield a saner guidance of life and help
to reduce the world's burden of suffering, injustice,
and callousness.   In this respect the second half of
that great millennium was particularly fruitful.   The
cult of the goddess of love and maternity, which had
had such picturesque developments in Syria, had led

to two new attitudes of the mind of the race. The
more admirable of these was that when the Greeks
and other Aryan peoples came into contact with this
cult in Asia Minor they generally discarded the
excesses of its love-temples, but eagerly adopted its
assurance that all men are brothers under the mother-
hood of the great earth-goddess. It is a large and as
yet little-known development—Sir W. Ramsay, a
Christian historian, has rendered fine service in trac-
ing it—and I must here be content to say that from
Lydia and the Greek cities of Asia Minor there spread
over the whole Greco-Roman world a spirit of friend-
liness, of good-fellowship, of brotherhood which
alleviated the lot of millions of people.

There were, especially, two ways in which the new
spirit exerted an active influence. It passed into the
philosophies of Zeno and Epicurus, who derived their
doctrine of the brotherhood of men from Asia Minor.
There are foolish attempts to show that Christianity,
which reached the Greco-Roman world along the same
path more than three centuries later, must have been
more effective because it mingled with the common
folk from whom the learned philosophers were isolated.
Those who speak thus wrongly imagine that students
of Greek philosophy were always as remote from the
crowd as were Plato and Aristotle. On the contrary,
philosophers at times dominated cities in the Greek
world, and their systems guided jurists and inspired
rulers. And no philosophy was so effective as the
blend of a Stoicism relieved of its mysticism and
asceticism, and an Epicureanism applied to daily life
which became the chief inspiration of the later Greco-

Roman world. Professor Gilbert Murray observes that " all the principal kings in existence in the generations following Zeno professed themselves Stoics," and it is a commonplace of history that under the Stoic emperors of Rome social idealism was borne to the highest point it had yet attained. In both cases, but especially the latter, the inspiration was a humanist blend of the Stoic and Epicurean philosophies.

The second practical issue was the establishment of innumerable little local groups of brotherly-minded and mutually-helpful workers. In all cities from Asia Minor to Italy the tanners, bakers, smiths, sailors, etc., had their " clubs " or " unions," as we now say, with meeting-rooms, benevolent funds, and periodical gay suppers. Each club had its patron deity and had a statue of the god or goddess in the meeting-room. Here brotherhood was the law. Women and slaves were, as the inscriptions tell, admitted with the free workers, and wealthy patrons often built the clubhouse. Both these outcomes of the brotherhood-spirit had spread over the Greco-Roman world before Christianity left its cradle. The barbaric features of the law were removed or softened by Stoic jurists. The condition of the slave was alleviated. Woman was relieved of her disabilities. Education was continuously extended, and many of the harsher features of old Roman life—which, let us not forget, was only a few centuries removed from barbarism—were obliterated or subjected to increasing criticism.

These developments had begun before Christianity was born and had proceeded far before it had the least social influence. But first let us notice another effect of the hectic cult of the love-goddess in and around Syria. By reaction it gave birth to a number of ascetic religions and moralities which stressed the sense of sin or shame, the need of purification, the contamination of sexual indulgence. Mithraism, and the new and ascetic cult of Isis from Egypt, which were both religions of this character, had their temples in Rome and Italy two centuries before the Roman Christians had the most modest sort of meeting-place, and the former swept the Roman world as far as Britain. Later came from Asia Minor the Manichæan religion, which was even more ascetic and redemptive. These religions were at hand on every side, as well as the teaching of the more austere Stoics, to meet the needs of the more mystic and the puritanical.

The Christian religion sprang from the same Persian root. Not differing from any of the rival religions and moralities, from the new and more humane Judaism of the first century to the teaching of the latest wandering moralist, in the sentiments of justice, kindliness, and mercy which were the common idealist property of the age, it had nevertheless a message of personal asceticism which was in some ways peculiar to itself. Unlike the Manichæan religion, which clung to the Persian dogma that the devil had created matter (and therefore the flesh), it modified this by using the old Semitic legend that the devil had perverted what God had made pure. This enabled it to retain the strict Persian horror of the flesh, and it seems to have been even more faithful than Manichæanism to the second outstanding dogma of the old Persian religion : that God would on some unknown day destroy the world, judge all men, and punish the wicked ever-lastingly. Moreover, it started from some Jewish preacher, probably the Jesus of the gospels, who, apparently after years of brooding in an Essenian monastery, in which Persian and Jewish ideas met, became convinced that this end of the world was at hand, and a man must rid himself of the material entanglements of wealth and love to prepare for the judgment or, as the Persian bible calls it on every page, the coming of the Kingdom of God.

The efforts of some of our Modernist theologians to prove that Jesus did not preach this doctrine incur the scorn of other, and not conservative, divines. The passages in which Jesus threatens men with eternal fire are, on the principles of the Modernists themselves, amongst the very oldest and presumably most authentic in the Gospels; and the generally accepted letters of Paul, which are held to be still earlier, are afire with the doctrine. And this one entirely distinctive doctrine of the new religion, while it should inspire a particularly fervent zeal for indi-vidual purity and virtue, ought to restrain any man from looking to it for a social ethic. It is, in fact, only under the pressure of our sceptical and socially-minded age that these books and sermons on the social inspiration of Jesus began to appear, and they were successful in their appeal only because, until we started a real science of comparative religion and un-earthed the religious literature of Egypt and Baby-lonia, most people wrongly believed that Christianity differed from other religions in its stress on justice, charity, and mutual aid.

This new zeal for a social ethic went so far that some of our more radical clergy began to find the germs of Socialism or Communism, as well as of pacifism and other modern ideals, in the sentiments of the early Christians. We have made no new discovery about early Christianity, and we are as far as ever from certainty about the shadowy figure that is reflected in the late and contradictory pages of the Gospels, but even ecclesiastical historians now read their documents more candidly. The familiar picture of the early Christian groups as Communist and frugal colonies, oases of fragrant virtue, in the rich and wicked cities of the Greco-Roman world, is a false description of their life even in the days of Paul, the earliest period in which we have a tolerably certain, though not wholly undisputed, glimpse of " followers of Christ."

The two groups of which Paul's scanty domestic references afford the best knowledge are those of Rome and Corinth. The group at Corinth gave Paul constant concern. In what we call his First Epistle to them, though he says in it that he has rebuked them in an earlier letter, we read that for some reason, which we plausibly assume to be their relative wealth, they will not expel members even for incest (v, 1).

Others of the group continue, despite his protests, to attend the meals given in honour of the gods in the temples. It appears that this is one of the wealthiest, or least poor, of the communities. They have paid teachers of religion, and they send funds to the poorer community at Jerusalem. Of communism and soli-

darity in virtue there is no question. And the letter
sent to them by the Romans under Clement at the
end of the century tells us that the Corinthian Church
is still of poor character.

The very small community at Rome, in the shipping and foreign quarter by the quays, was just as far
removed from Socialism. Paul, writing to them about
the year 55, sends his greetings to those members who
are " of Narcissus's people " (the correct translation)
and others " of Aristobulus's people." The phrase
suggests, as Duchesne says, that they are clients, or
middle-class dependants, of two rich Romans ; for
Narcissus was the most powerful courtier of the
Emperor Claudius, even if a freedman, and Aristobulus was a friend of the Emperor and grandson of
King Herod. Indeed, writing from Rome to the
Philippians in the days of Nero, Paul sends greetings
from " those who are of the Emperor's people " ; and
Paul was not in the habit of sending the compliments
of slaves. The First Epistle to Timothy is now
ascribed by many to an unknown author—if it were
not in the Bible we should say forger—of the end of
the century, though others still regard it as written
by Paul before the year 65. It indicates that some in
the community are rich, and it merely urges them to
be generous.

In short, it is absurdly unhistorical to take a temporary practice of the very poor group at Jerusalem
which lived largely on alms from the other churches,
and call this Primitive Christianity. As Dr. Shirley
J. Case, who nevertheless contrives to see radical social
and political aims in the new religion (ignoring the

expectation of a speedy end of the world), points out, the little groups consisted of men and women of every class, the poorer workers meeting with the others in the homes of those who were rich enough to have large rooms. Apart from their ritual Communion Supper, they had periodical convivial suppers, and naturally the comfortable members shared their good food with the very poor. You may see it done in a parochial picnic to-day.

There is, in any case, no question of a social influence of the new religion on the Roman world before the fourth century, when the Emperor began to profess the Christian faith. Orthodox folk used to imagine that the new religion made a deep impression on the pagans because of the heroism with which tens of thousands of martyrs endured torture and death. But the tortures and other details of the old legends are so comically foreign to Roman life that a higher criticism of this amazing branch of literature began centuries ago. Now even Catholic scholars like the Jesuit Father Delehaye and Dr. Ehrhard tell us that almost the whole of these martyr-stories are either pure fiction or romances based upon a grain of obscure fact. The more popular the martyr (George, Agnes, Catherine, Cæcilia, Denis, Laurence, Sebastian, etc.) and the more picturesque the story, the more certain it is to be fictitious. Very few records of martyrdoms are now accepted as genuine.

The truth is that in the two (not seven) general persecutions of Christians, for definite political reasons, almost the entire body apostatized. It is, for instance, claimed—excessively, I estimate—that there were

50,000 Christians at Rome when Decius ordered the first general persecution. Now, the Catholic Professor Ehrhard says, approvingly, of the work of his Jesuit colleague :

He puts *all* accounts of Roman martyrs in the third class of Acts of Martyrs, which we may describe as religious romances (*Die altchristliche Literatur*, p. 556).

In a special small work Father Delehaye has shown that no Christians were ever exposed to the lions in the Roman amphitheatre. In fact, we can hardly trace a score of Roman martyrs in the Decian persecution, and thus nearly the whole body rushed to offer incense at the pagan altars or bribe officials to certify that they had done so.

Hence the claim of moral influence in this respect is entirely mythical and is based upon stories which were forged by the thousand at Rome in the early part of the Dark Age. And an outline of the history of the Roman Church—I have written it in full elsewhere— the only branch of the Church which could conceivably exercise any other social influence, will suffice to show that there is no question of such influence before the age of Constantine.

That the little group grew in numbers and virtue for a few years under the personal supervision of Paul in the days of Nero, and that there was then a persecution in which Paul (though certainly not Peter) was executed, I accept as historical facts ; chiefly on the ground of the Roman tradition which appears in Clement's Letter to the Corinthians thirty years later. The forged reference in Tacitus to " an immense number of Christians " I, of course, do not accept. It was a group that could gather round the fiery apostle in some private house in the poor suburb across the Tiber. If we accepted the Roman tradition that Nero's wife Poppæa—as vicious a woman as that morbid age produced—was a Christian, and that a few years later the patrician Flavius Clemens and his wife joined the sect, we get far away from the picture of an austere communist group. But Roman literature is drenched with forgery about the first three centuries.

What we do know, for it is recorded in the official annals (the Pontifical Calendar), is that the Roman Christians still met in private houses until the year 220, when they secured the room above a poor wine-shop, and for the first time bought a few silver cups. About this time the community grew very much larger, and it discarded the last trace of austerity. It is a contemporary Roman bishop, Hippolytus, the one scholar whom the Roman Church produced in many centuries and a man of strict character, who tells the sordid story. Pope Callistus, a wily and greedy ex-slave, enjoyed the favour of the leading lady of the immense and utterly revolting harem of the Emperor Commodus, Marcia, who had been reared to her trade by a Christian eunuch. It is enough here to say that Callistus repealed the church-law which excluded grave sinners, and numbers of wealthy and vicious Roman ladies joined the sect.

This was the body which, in thirty years of toleration, grew to, on my estimate, about 20,000 at the most, and was scattered by the first wind of persecution. The African Father, Tertullian, whose

Church offered far more martyrs in this Decian persecution, speaks with the bitterest disdain of the Romans.   However, in the ensuing peace the Church was restored, and in a further forty years of toleration it came once more to number about 20,000. This, we must remember, was in a city of about a million people ; and, as the Greek language was used in the ritual and the Popes were nonentities with no supporters of any distinction, it would be absurd to inquire if they had any influence on the life of Rome or the Empire.

In the first decade of the fourth century the great Emperor Diocletian ordered the destruction of Christianity.   He is the first emperor who had Christians in his family and in high positions in his palace and army.   But, instead of this giving them an influence on Roman life, they provoked by their insolence the drastic persecution which again sent all but a score or so of the 20,000 Roman Christians to the pagan altars. Doubtless hundreds did linger in the subterranean catacombs, but we now perceive that these became the burying-place of ordinary Christians in the peace that followed, and it was the profit of the traffic in relics, which began half a century later, that converted most of these into " martyrs."   By 305 Christianity was in ruins.   But seven years later the cross glittered at the head of Constantine's armies at the gates of Rome, and from this point we begin a serious study of the social record of Christianity.

CHAPTER II

HOW ANCIENT SLAVERY ENDED

LET me first stress the importance of making this chronological point clear. In support of the myth that the new religion brought into the Roman world a higher ideal of conduct it was customary to paint the Romans, before they were touched by the Christian ethic, in the darkest colours. Nine-tenths of the readers knew nothing of Roman history, and you could quote the horrors of the short reigns of Caligula or Nero, and even borrow Mommsen's sombre description of Roman life eighty years before Jesus was born, to convey an impression of the kind of vice which Christianity regenerated. It is therefore material to understand that, whatever periods of decay or license there may have been in Roman history before the fourth century, this has nothing to do with the influence of Christianity.

One historical fact ought to puzzle any man or woman who still cherishes the legend. Six years before Jesus was born, as that date is now generally conceived, the Emperor Augustus took so stern a step in the interest of virtue that it has scarcely a parallel in the lives of rulers. The law of these wicked Romans punished adultery with death. You may, in fact, find it amusing to tell your simple-minded Christian friend, who believes that the Babylonians and the Romans were the most licentious of all peoples, that they were almost the only two great nations who in their law imposed the death-penalty for adultery. Happily, it was not usually applied, but Augustus set the law in motion against the smart set of Rome, and, when he was convinced that his beautiful and dearly-loved daughter Julia was one of the sinners, he, in spite of the entreaties of all Rome, banished her to a desolate island and, when an attempt was made to release her, confined her for life in a rigorous prison.

This aspect of Roman life does not specially concern me here, but it is part of the general social appreciation, and it will be useful to outline Roman history to the accession of Constantine. From the date of the accession of Augustus and his wife, two admirable rulers, to that of the death of Marcus Aurelius—a period of nearly two hundred years—the Empire was governed by, with few exceptions, as fine a body of men as the annals of any nation will show over such a period. The morbid reigns of Caligula, Nero, and Domitian, upon which so much rhetoric is expended, occupied only, collectively, thirty years out of the two hundred.

Moreover, in the second half of this period, before even the most sanguine enthusiast looks for Christian influence, the Empire was ruled for ninety years by one of the finest known series of monarchs, the so-called Stoic (in reality Epicurean) emperors. Some distrust Gibbon when he says that this was the period when in all history the human race was " most happy and prosperous," but a greater (and Christian) authority on Roman morals, Friedlaender, tells us that it was " an age which roused itself by its own effort to higher and purer views of morality than all the ages which preceded it" (*Roman Life and Manners*, III, 280) ; and Mr. T. R. Glover, the most learned of living Christian apologists as regards Roman history, says that " the second century A.D. was perhaps the period when a greater proportion of the civilized world had a better government than at any other time " (*The Influence of Christ in the Ancient World*, p. 13).   The title of Glover's book may wrongly suggest that he here finds Christian influence.   On the contrary, even his claim of influence at a later date is of the vaguest and feeblest description.

After the death of Marcus Aurelius, who was the only real Stoic but socially the least effective of the " Stoic emperors," the Empire broke into disorder, and there were alternate good and bad or weak rulers for a century.   But Diocletian restored the Empire and its social idealism just before Constantine fought his way to the throne.   Further, all the bribery (money-gifts, promotion, etc.) and pressure that Constantine used could not bring more than a minority to the Church, and it cost his successors fifty years of drastic persecution and suppression of all other religions to convert this minority into a majority. Until then, apart from a certain influence of the bishops on legislation, which we shall see, there is no question of broad Christian action.   It is the Romans of the middle or second half of the fourth century whom we have to consider in connection with the sup-

posed social effects of the Christian religion.   And, as
such special studies of fourth-century life as that of
Sir Samuel Dill (a Protestant) make clear, the Romans
had now reached a degree of sobriety and refinement
which Christian Europe would not again reach until
the nineteenth century.   The tone of the patrician
class in general was so altered that they, as we read in
the *Saturnalia* of Macrobius, discussed with shocked
amazement the excesses of the earlier Romans.   The
mass of the people had free schools everywhere, as we
shall see, woman was free and respected, and men
still enjoyed the more humane law and the remarkable system of philanthropy which the Stoics had
created.

It may be necessary to explain, briefly, that the
Empire did not owe this to its new Christian emperors.
Constantine and his dynasty are as deeply stained
with blood and vice as any short dynasty in European
history.   Constantine had his wife and his illegitimate
son murdered, apparently for incest—for that the
Romans drove him to build and live in Constantinople
—and an orgy of murder for the succession followed
his death.   In short, twelve princes of his house were
murdered and 100,000 men slain in their civil wars in
the twenty years' struggle that followed.   The only
member of the dynasty whom historians fully respect,
Julian, renounced the new religion with disgust.

But this improved Roman civilization still had profound social evils, and an exact inquiry into the extent
and character of the influence of Christianity must
consider whether, or how far, it conquered or modified
these.   The worst was that the Empire was based on

slavery.   The several hundred thousand free citizens of Rome had a more pampered life than the workers have ever had or have in any other civilization.   They received a free supply of corn for their staple food, free medical service, a free and excellent supply of water, and free schooling.   They had the most superb free entertainments, sometimes costing nearly £100,000 in a day, in the Circus and Amphitheatre, and their almost free baths were immense marble palaces with spacious and beautiful halls, libraries, and gymnasia. By the laws of Diocletian they were awarded a minimum wage ; and it is again piquant to notice that the Babylonians alone can be coupled with them in this measure of justice.   And, instead of the Christian day of rest being, as ignorant apologists imagine, a welcome novelty to them, they worked on only about 170 days of the 365.   The rest were holidays, and hundreds of millions had been spent on building palatial baths, marble colonnades, amphitheatres, theatres, and circuses for them.   The Great Circus, which held nearly 400,000 of them, gave them a free show, of the finest bloodless entertainment then known, on a hundred full days a year.   From this height of freedom and enjoyment the workers of the Roman world were within less than a century of the establishment of Christianity to be cast down to a level of sordid poverty, heavy toil, and virtual slavery.

This pampered existence was, however, based on the labours of millions of slaves ; the men of alien race, generally war-captives and their descendants, who raised the free corn and toiled in the mines and galleys

and industries.   How many there were in the fourth
century no one has the least idea.   At one time it was
said that in the Greco-Roman world there were many
times—one writer said thirty times—as many slaves
as free men.   All recent experts cut down these older
figures and point out that the material from which we
can make any estimate is very unreliable.   In the
most recent authoritative work on the subject, *Slavery
in the Roman Empire* (1928), Mr. R. H. Barrow gives
three expert estimates of the number of slaves in the
city of Rome :

Marquardt	.	710,000 free, 900,000 slaves.
Beloch	.	520,000 free, 280,000 slaves.
Kahrstedt	.	781,000 free, 200,000 slaves.

Marquardt's estimate is the oldest and has long been
discarded.   Kahrstedt's is one of the latest (1920)
and most scientific ; and it fairly agrees with Kühn's
estimate that of the industrial workers of the whole of
Italy 75 per cent were free.   Probably we should say
that the best opinion to-day is that in Greece, where
slaves were, as a rule, not badly treated until Christian
times, the free and enslaved workers were about equal
in number ; while in the Western or Roman half of
civilization the slaves may have been at some time
twice as numerous.

   But here the question of date is again important.
The great mass of the Roman slaves in the days when
they were most numerous were war-captives, mainly
Teutons and Slavs.   The Romans, let me repeat, were
only a few centuries out of barbarism in the days of
Cæsar, and it was possible to represent that enslaving

a captive was a humane advance upon the barbaric practice of cutting his throat.   That is, in fact, how apologists explain the similar practice of the Hebrews, unrebuked by any moralist in the Old Testament. And the formidable wars of the Romans in the second and first centuries B.C. had brought vast numbers of captives to Rome.   A single frontier war would yield 100,000.   But all experts recognize that this chief source of slavery shrank materially from the beginning of the Christian Era, and the numbers of slaves fell.   The last great haul was Titus's capture of 97,000 Jews.   Glover observes that from the second century A.D. onward there was a scarcity of slaves.   Barrow, who has probably made more careful research than any, says that by the end of the second century A.D. the great slave-tilled estates, their chief area of work, were considerably reduced.   In other words, the worst days of slavery were long over when, in the fourth century, Christianity began to rule the minds of princes and of slave-owners.

Barrow says that, apart from the shrinkage of the main source of slaves, " slavery failed because it was expensive and inefficient and was gradually realized to be so " (*Slavery in the Roman Empire*, p. 97).   We shall see that this is one of the real causes of the great reduction of slavery—it was not " abolished " until the nineteenth century—in the ancient world which the modern historian or sociologist gives us instead of the old type of moral rhetoric, but let us first realize that the condition of the slave also had been profoundly altered long before there was any Christian influence.   By all means let us be reminded of the brutalities of some of the earlier Romans : of the way in which the slaves on the great estates were treated worse than cattle, of the irresponsible cruelty of masters and mistresses in some of the mansions, and so on.   Much of this is exaggerated.   When we are told, for instance, how in fits of temper patricians would fling their slaves to the fishes in their ponds, we should know that only one such master is known ; and he was certainly not a Stoic as Dr. Harrison makes him.   Nor do the apologists go on to tell how, when the Emperor learned this practice of Vedius Pollio, he had his fish-ponds and bowls destroyed.   The case is mentioned with burning indignation by Seneca (*De Clementia*, I, 18), and that moralist induced the Emperor to pass a law compelling magistrates to examine charges of cruelty brought against their masters by slaves.

Here, in fact, is in brief the record of these " callous pagans " in connection with slavery.   In 82 B.C. the Cornelian Law forbade the murder of slaves.   Fifty years later the Petronian Law forbade masters to send slaves to fight in the amphitheatre.   With the close of the civil wars and the founding of the Empire—still twenty years before the birth of Christ—there was an improved moral tone, as all historians find ; and, when short periods of debasement led again to excesses, Seneca induced Nero, while he still had influence over him, to pass the law protecting the slave from cruelty. Like every other Stoic and Epicurean teacher, Seneca pleaded for the kindly treatment of slaves.   In one of his letters (XLVII) he exclaims : " Slaves ! No, lowly friends."   It is a repetition of the words of Epicurus himself.

There then opened, as we saw, the ninety-years period of the Stoic emperors, and, short of abolishing slavery, everything that was possible was done for the slave.   Since we are now told that the reason why Jesus, Paul, and every Christian writer or leader for a thousand years refrained from condemning slavery was that they saw that it was economically impossible to abolish it—as if Jesus and Paul ever glanced at the economic order—we shall hardly blame the emperors for not doing so.   Yet the pagan moralists did condemn it and demand its abolition.   Now that the Orations of Dio Chrysostom are available in English any person may verify this.   He was the greatest orator of his age (about A.D. 100), a warm friend of the Emperor and of great influence with the aristocracy. Yet in his fourteenth and fifteenth Orations, which were delivered in a public hall in the Forum at Rome, he explicitly and at great length condemned slavery as unjust.   About the same time lived Pliny the Younger, and from his extant letters (VIII, 16, etc.) we learn that even the agricultural slaves were now treated with consideration.   The Emperor Hadrian, an Epicurean, suppressed the practice of housing slaves underground, renewed the laws which punished the murderer of a slave or the master who sent them to the amphitheatre, and banished a wealthy lady for cruelty to her slaves.   The Emperor Antoninus Pius decreed that if a slave fled from a cruel master and embraced an altar or a statue of the Emperor, he should go free.

It is in reference to this prolonged period of social idealism that Sir Samuel Dill, who gives us a masterly study of it in his *Roman Society from Nero to Marcus Aurelius*, says that " the slave class of antiquity really corresponded to our free labouring class " (p. 18).   In the same appreciative vein he describes pagan life in the fourth century in his *Roman Society in the Last Century of the Western Empire*.   And we must not suppose that in the troubled intervening period the social idealism of the Romans perished.   To the third century belongs the famous Stoic jurist Ulpianus, who explicitly denounced slavery as " against the law of nature " and induced the Emperor Caracalla to forbid parents to sell their children into slavery.   The Emperor Diocletian, in fine, forbade men to sell themselves into slavery and made it illegal to enslave a man for debt.

These facts, which may be verified in any recent manual on ancient slavery, show how profoundly unjust the older apologists were to the Romans and constitute a splendid social record of the Stoic-Epicurean philosophy which inspired them.   What, on the other hand, is the record of Christianity ?   Against the outrageous claim, which is still repeated in some apologetic works and in sermons, that Christianity " broke the fetters of the slave " I will now show two facts :

1. Neither the Christian Church nor any Christian body ever condemned slavery until modern times.
2. Ancient slavery decayed from economic reasons, but slavery was never abolished until the sceptical nineteenth century.

It is a miserable subterfuge to say that Jesus, Paul, and the Christian Fathers condemned slavery " implicitly," for in that case it was condemned by every

moralist who ever lived.   It is frankly ridiculous to
say that they were restrained from condemning it out
of concern for the Roman economic world, for such a
consideration is completely foreign to their minds.
And it is futile to quote passages in which they urge
the humane treatment of slaves, for every moralist
had done this.   The plain fact is that down to the year
1000—what happened later we shall see—no Christian
leader, much less a Pope or Council, condemned
slavery.   The only attempt to reply to this statement
of mine that I have seen is a claim, in a stupid little
booklet published by the Christian Evidence Society,
that Gregory of Nyssa condemned slavery.   The
writer must have known, since he quoted the words,
that the book in question is published in the Migne
edition of the Fathers with an express warning that
leading authorities regard it as spurious.   It has all
the appearance of having been written by an ex-slave
monk.

But there is a worse vice in apologetic literature on
this subject.   The writers have roamed through the
vast library of the works of the Fathers in search of
passages urging the humane treatment of slaves, but I
do not know a single one of them who has quoted the
words of St. Augustine, the greatest and most influential of the Fathers, and the only one who candidly
faces the issue of the *justice* of slavery.   This passage,
moreover, is in Augustine's most famous work, *The
City of God*, which is translated into every European
language.   The fifteenth chapter of Book XIX deals
with slavery, *and defends it*.   God created men free,
but they sinned, and slavery is a just punishment in

his sight.   He says (to translate literally from the
Latin) :

> The first cause of slavery, then, is sin—that a man should
> be put in bonds by another ; and this happens only by the
> judgment of God, in whose eyes it is no crime.

A Protestant historian, Dr. Emil Reich, who particularly studied Rome, sternly condemned apologists of
all schools for their libels of the Romans.   On our
present point he says :

> It is an historical fact, supported by the most positive of
> evidence, that slavery in the Roman Empire was mitigated
> by the noble philosophy of the Stoics and not by the teach-
> ing of the Church Fathers, who never thought of recommend-
> ing the abolition of slavery (*History of Civilization*, p. 421).

As we now see, Dr. Reich did not go far enough.   The
one Father who faced the issue, the one who had immeasurably the greatest influence, said that slavery
was just.   He expressly repudiated the Stoic claim.
    What, then, do apologists who have some know-
ledge of history say in extenuation of this complete
moral failure of the Church in face of the gravest social
malady of the ancient world ?   In the *Encyclopædia
of Religion and Ethics* the Rev. Dr. L. D. Agate writes
the article on Slavery and says (p. 604) :

> The general impression left by the attitude of the Church
> is that it tended to make slavery milder, though not to
> abolish it, and, owing to its excessive care for the rights
> of the masters, *even to perpetuate what would otherwise have
> passed away.*

In the first part of this we readily acquiesce, in the
sense that, like the pagan moralists (as Dr. Agate

ought to have said), really religious Christians recommended humanity.   But if the words are understood to mean that the Christian Emperors made any further legal reform of the institution of slavery, we cannot admit them.   Dr. Agate reminds us that Constantine, unlike some of his pagan predecessors (who feared a conspiracy of freedmen), encouraged the manumission (freeing) of slaves.   Yes, as a reward of conversion to Christianity ; but this same Constantine undid some of the reforms by again permitting parents to sell their children into slavery, allowing the finder of an exposed child to rear it as a slave, and decreeing that if a Christian woman had intercourse with a slave both should be put to death.

The apologist Mr. Brace (*Gesta Christi*) says that the Emperor Gratian passed a law giving freedom to slaves who informed against " those guilty of certain capital offences."   The truth is that Gratian offered liberty to slaves who gave information about *plots against himself*, but he ordered that they be burned alive—a barbarity unknown to the pagan emperors—if they brought any other charge against their masters. Next Mr. Brace tells how Justinian ordered that slaves be decently married.   It is rather ironic to boast that this was done only two hundred years after the triumph of Christianity (by imperial decree) in the Greek world—they had meantime continued to be coupled like cattle—but, as Dean Milman showed long ago, this new slave-arrangement was not regarded by the Church as real marriage until the ninth century. Dr. Agate asks us to admire how Justinian in his famous Code echoes the feeling of the Stoic jurists that slavery was " against the law of nature." But he would have found on closer inquiry that this Code was compiled, not by the hand of Justinian himself, but by the last of the great pagan jurists, Tribonian.

By this time, the sixth century, the vast ancient system of slavery in Europe was in ruins. But this was not due to the pressure of moralists of any school. The system fell, inevitably, with the economic fabric of which it was a part. The barbarians wrecked the Empire, annihilated the government that had controlled millions of public slaves, and destroyed the fortunes of the wealthy. No man was left who could, as in the old days, own his thousands of slaves. In the year 300 there were probably still 20,000,000 slaves in Europe, but in the sixth century there were not 10,000,000 people of all classes and ages. Thus ancient slavery, the slavery of tens of millions, was destroyed by notorious economic causes.

It would now have been comparatively easy to abolish slavery. In the appalling chaos of the fifth century the troops of slaves first broke away and dispersed, then, owing to the famine-conditions, returned to serve wherever labour was reorganized. The barbaric chiefs and their " nobles," and the decayed gentlefolk who survived here and there in country mansions, were all Christians. But the only words that fell from consecrated lips were as harsh as ever. The contemporary priest Salvianus tells us that the Christians treated their slaves worse than the pagans had done. Paulinus of Pella quite naïvely admits that men of his class, survivors of the old nobility, regarded it as no sin to have intercourse with their

female slaves.   The churches and monasteries owned
slaves.   The greatest Pope of the fifth century, Leo
the Great, aristocratically ruled that no slave could
become a cleric lest his " vileness " should " pollute "
the sacred order ; and it is only by omitting the word
" pollute " that apologists can pretend that *vilitas*
does not mean " vileness."   The greatest Pope of the
sixth century, Gregory the Great, was the richest
slave-owner in Europe and forbade slaves to marry
free Christian women.   Ingram quotes Gregory saying that slavery is " against nature," and would have
us believe that this " celebrated declaration " represented " the general attitude of the priesthood toward
slavery."   If he had read Gregory's letter (VI, 12)
more carefully, he would have seen that the Pope is
merely freeing two slaves who have money and
promise to leave it to the Church.   No case is recorded
in which he freed one of his tens of thousands of slaves
without payment.   So the great crime was sustained.
We will resume the story in the fourth chapter, and
we shall find with Dr. Agate—who says only what the
Catholic historian Muratori had shown in detail long
ago—that the attitude of the Church " tended to per-
petuate what would otherwise have passed away."
Slavery is the last word that any Christian apologist
ought to mention.

CHAPTER III

EDUCATION AND THE POSITION OF WOMAN

WITHIN the limitations of this book it will not be possible to examine at equal length all the claims of the apologists. I have dwelt at length on this issue of slavery because it was the most terrible evil of the ancient world, and because not a manual of apologetics appears without renewing the claim in some form, while the more popular books and sermons still affirm quite blatantly that Christianity abolished slavery. The facts are now given in a dozen special historical works on slavery, and one is amazed at the persistent refusal of so many religious writers to consult them. But the second and third major claims of the apologist—that the new religion gave the world schools and uplifted women—are equally, if not more reckless. One can rhetorically plead that the Christian principle of brotherhood *must* have helped the slaves ; especially if one is ignorant that it was not in the least distinctive of the new religion and that such divines as Augustine declared it to be quite consistent with slavery. One might even argue, if one ignores the historical facts, that the Christian teaching *must* have uplifted woman. But the claim, which few apologists omit, that Christianity promoted education is a particularly audacious defiance of the facts and is not even involved in Christian principles.

The truth may now be read in a dozen manuals of the history of education (Compayré, Boyd, Duggan, Monroe, etc.), and about the broad facts there is no dispute. The life of St. Augustine alone ought to inform any man how splendid was the system of education, comparatively to earlier ages, the Roman Empire had created. Practically all the children of the free workers had gratuitous elementary instruction, for the law compelled the municipalities to provide schools, and there was a very liberal provision of free secondary or " grammar " schools. Augustine, born in the year 354, found schools of both types in the small Roman-African town in which his parents lived. A network of them covered the Empire. Then there were many higher or university schools—Augustine attended one at Carthage—to which selected youths of sixteen passed, and the poorer had not to pay. And besides these there were, in cities like Rome, Milan, and Carthage, large numbers of private colleges —one on the Capitol at Rome had thirty masters— which were so frequented by sons of the wealthier that the more famous teachers made about £4,000 a year. At Alexandria were the most famous schools of all, in which Greek science and philosophy still sheltered until the monks murdered the great teacher, Hypatia, in 415 because she disdainfully refused, in spite of the law, to profess to be a Christian. At Athens the old schools of philosophy kept the flag of Greek culture flying until Justinian suppressed them in the sixth century.

These facts are now as securely established as the wars of Julius Cæsar, and it is equally well known to historians of education that the Church was, quite naturally, bitterly opposed to the entire system.   The schools were almost wholly occupied with pagan literature.   Very few of the better-educated Romans would join the Church, as Augustine complains, and the great schools of Alexandria and Athens were the last strongholds of the free spirit.   To protect its own youth, especially in learned Alexandria, the Church had been compelled to open a few religious schools; but to tell the public that Christianity " gave the world schools " is, in view of the Roman system I have just described, a confession of remarkable ignorance.

This fine educational system of the Empire inevitably perished in the general political and economic collapse, and we need not enlarge on the way in which Christian mobs, led by monks or bishops, hacked and burned the last lingering traces of it.   And it need not be said that in view of the terrible impoverishment of Europe after 450 it was quite impossible to set up a new educational system, in which the works of Jerome and Augustine might replace the pagan classics.   So much we grant, but the conditions of the time do not in the least explain this appalling fact : that during the next five centuries you could count on your fingers the number of schools that existed in the whole of Europe in any generation.   D. W. Boyd, who is far from anti-clerical, says in his *History of Western Education* (1921) that we cannot trace the existence of a single school in Europe in the year 500. Denk, who holds that the best-preserved province was

Gaul, has given us the results of his laborious research in the literature of that province (*Geschichte des Gallo-Frankischen Unterrichts*). Yet in the sixth and later centuries he finds only a few little schools, and these give only religious instruction. With this Dr. J. B. Mullinger, who has covered the ground from 450 to 850 in his *Schools of Charles the Great*, entirely agrees. Only a few schools for teaching priests and monks existed, and even these were in decay when, in 789, Charlemagne ordered the bishops and the monks to open schools. How many were opened we have not the least idea, but we do know that the bishops closed them as soon as Charlemagne died, and the people of Europe remained illiterate and weirdly ignorant to the extent of 99 per cent until about 1100. Apart from small and temporary local enthusiasms, that was the condition of Europe generally. What happened from 1100 onward we shall see later.

For these facts, on which the educational experts are agreed, we obviously require some other explanation than the fall of Rome. And it is easy : the Church opposed education and disdained secular learning. To rebut this some writers quote the Christian schools and scholars of Alexandria—not mentioning that, as Origen says, they were shamed into doing something by the pagan taunts of their boorishness—and the early works of Augustine. The truth is that Augustine, when he became a bishop, scorned all learning, called Plato " a fool," and taught that " it is the ignorant who enter heaven." I have traced his degeneration in my *St. Augustine and His Age.* Tertullian, Lactantius, Jerome, and other Latin Fathers were just as scornful.   Dr. H. A. Mann, in his *Lives of the Popes*, has the audacity to quote praise of learning from a work that purports to have been written by Gregory the Great.   Not only is this work admitted to be a forgery, but we have a genuine letter (XI, 54) in which Gregory sternly rebukes a French bishop for opening a school for secular learning, and calls his action " horrible " and " execrable."   According to John of Salisbury it was Gregory who burned at Rome the last collections of the older Roman works.

That is another aspect of the work of the Church. Libraries of from 100,000 to 700,000 books existed in the Greco-Roman cities until the fifth century, preserving all that the race had won in science, philosophy, and history.   They were all destroyed by the Christians.   The largest of them all, that of Alexandria, was destroyed by the same monks and mob who murdered Hypatia ; for the story that this library was burned three centuries later by the Arabs is a very late and now discredited fiction.   All that was preserved in Europe of Greek science were a few badly garbled fragments in the school manuals of one or two Italian writers.   Thus the most promising of all human developments was stifled, and it was from the East that the Persians and Arabs had four centuries later, to get the works which inspired them to resume the study of science.   Any man who asks us to be grateful to the Church because Cassiodorus or Martianus Capella preserved a few crumbs of Greek science while their fellow-Christians destroyed all the rest must have the apologetic type of mind.

As to the fiction that the monks preserved the

classics for us, it is now mildewed in every serious library. Catholic writers still repeat the assurance of their superficial Montalembert that "without these copyists we should possess nothing—absolutely nothing—of classical antiquity." But the highest authority on the subject, Professor Heeren, finds that there was not a monastery in Europe that "rendered any service whatever in connection with classical literature" (*Geschichte des Studiums der classischen Literatur*, p. 101). It is now agreed that of the vast whole of Greek literature only one work of Aristotle at the most was preserved in Europe, and any student ought to know that the "preservation" of the Latin classics was such that at the Renaissance it took scholars a hundred years of industrious search to get together a partial collection of them. It is rather silly to imagine really religious monks preserving for the world the works of Terence, Plautus, Ovid, Martial, Horace, Catullus, etc., which are now offered us as proof of the indecency of the Romans ; and the vast majority of the monks were idle and ignorant parasites. Compayré shows that at the end of the thirteenth century—the great period of the Catholic universities—there was not a single monk in the largest monastery in France, St. Gall, who could read and write. As to their libraries, about which so much nonsense is written, there was not a library in Christian Europe for a thousand years that contained 10,000 works, whereas the Alexandrian Library in the fourth century and the royal Arab library at Cordova in the tenth had each more than half a million.

Not much better is the claim that Christianity ren-

dered an invaluable service to the child by suppressing infanticide and the exposure of unwanted children.
Lecky's treatment of the former, which he calls " a
crying vice " of the Empire, is lamentable.   In support of this grave statement he gives only a few facts
scattered over many centuries.   There was no such
crying vice, certainly not after the first century.   On
the contrary, not only was it murder in Roman law,
but the killing of infants was precisely the most indignant charge that the pagans brought against the
Christians.

The exposure or leaving in public places of unwanted female infants, which would then be collected
by baby-farmers and reared for slavery or prostitution, was a more serious evil.   But the apologists even
here distort the facts.   Dr. Harrison illustrates " the
deadness of the Roman conscience on this subject "
by saying that the very character in Terence who
utters the familiar line, " I am a man, and nothing
human is alien from me," goes on to blame his wife for
exposing instead of killing their infant daughter (*All
That Jesus Began*, 1934, p. 66).   He might have mentioned that this was written 450 years before Constantine's accession, and that, as he ought to have noticed
in Lecky, from whom he borrowed the fact, Chremes,
the father in the play, scolded his wife because the
child would now be reared as a prostitute.   To a
Roman, not believing that a child had an immortal
soul, extinction in pre-conscious infancy seemed pre-
ferable to maintaining a life that was destined for
either slavery or prostitution.

We should certainly expect a religion which said,

not only that the infant had an immortal soul but a soul that could be damned for ever if it were not baptized and reared a Christian, to put an end to exposure. But there is not the least positive proof that it did. Dr. Harrison says that " it was not until the reign of Valentinian I (A.D. 364–75) that exposure was condemned as murder." But in one of the best authorities on the subject, Pauly's *Real-Encyclopädie* (article " Aussetzung "), we read that it is only a probable interpretation of the law of Valentinian and Valens that it imposed capital punishment for exposure as well as infanticide, and that the law had this effect only because the Stoic jurist Paulus had in the reign of Alexander Severus laid it down that the exposure of children was murder (*Dig.*, XXV, 3, 4). The passage of Paulus is given in Lecky (II, 12) and is singularly overlooked by Dr. Harrison, who has made so much use of Lecky. As to Dr. Harrison's " two hundred years of legislation on the subject between the days of Constantine and Justinian "—Constantine's only law was reactionary, and the only other was that of Valentinian—he must mean church-legislation, which is misleading. There is no historical evidence of a change in Roman practice after the establishment of Christianity, but we may assume that when, in the fifth century, the population of Rome and other cities fell to one-twentieth of what they had been, the practice would be reduced.

On the other hand, the claim that Christianity redeemed the Romans of their callousness by suppressing the gladiatorial games is a piece of rhetorical deceit. It is chiefly based upon a pretty story of a monk, Telemachus, throwing himself into the arena at Rome in protest. Those who repeat the story do not add that the monk is supposed to have been killed by the Christian mob, but the story is worthless. It is given by no Roman writer of the time—it is found first in a half-century later and unreliable Greek—and there is no St. Telemachus in Roman lists of martyrs. And it is historically false that the games were suppressed in 404 ; though even this is ninety years after the bishops began to have influence over the emperors. The games, which cost enormous sums, were doomed when the wealth of Rome was dissipated ; but Salvianus (VI, 2) describes them in Christian Gaul about 450, and in the East, where there was no invasion by barbarians, they lingered, like the indecent shows of the theatre, long afterwards. It is, in fact, almost humorous to make such a claim when, as everybody knows, animal-fights, duels (often consecrated as ordeals), bloody tournaments, etc., were amongst the most cherished diversions of the Middle Ages, and seeing that the Greeks had none of these barbarities until the Christian emperors introduced them.

Yet all these old claims are renewed every few years in apologetic literature, with a fine indifference to modern historical research. You find them in all their rustic health in C. D. Eldridge's *Christianity's Contribution to Civilization* (1929). You get the glorious story of Telemachus, the Christian mitigation of the horrors of slavery, the Christian suppression of infanticide and exposure, the Christian promotion of education, the Christian service of woman through " those enthusiastic champions of womanhood " the knights of the age of chivalry . . ." We shall see later what history and literature now have to say about the knights and their ladies. It would give a painful shock to our Eldridges. But the idea that at least the Church redeemed woman from some sort of dark indignities she had suffered in pagan days is so common that a page must be given to it.

The truth about the change in woman's position in Christendom has been candidly described so often, especially as most of our feminist historians were anti-clerical until the cause became prosperous and attracted the clergy, that the loyalty of our women to the Churches seems ironic. The broad truth is that, just as the millions of free literate workers of the pagan world were replaced by the massively illiterate serfs of the Middle Ages, so the free woman of Roman days gave place to a womanhood suffering atrocious disabilities, social and legal, from which the sex has been delivered only in the last century. In Egypt and Babylonia woman had been the equal of man, and we may almost say the same of the Hittite, Assyrian, Syrian, Cretan, and Phœnician women. In Judæa alone, in that ancient world, was she unjustly treated ; and now even a Labour daily gives its readers a series of articles on " Women of the Old Testament "— mostly fictitious—including a harlot who for a price betrayed her city.

The Greeks and Romans had begun with a tradition of masculine tyranny, but the women of the Greco-Roman world had won justice before Christianity was out of its swaddling clothes. Election-appeals signed by women in the first century were found on the walls of Pompeii, and women (Livia, Agrippina, Plotina, Julia Mamæa, etc.) played great parts in imperial history. In the fourth century the wives of the finer patricians, who were often priestesses of Isis, were independent and respected. They were angels in comparison with the types of women who would presently appear in Christian Gaul and Italy or in the Byzantine world. Greek ecclesiastical history particularly extols the Empress Theodora, the Empress " the most pious " Irene, and the Empress St. Theodora ; the first was an ex-prostitute of ungovernable temper and no scruples, the second had the eyes of her own son (and of thousands of others) cut out, and the third had her son educated in debauchery and her archbishop blinded.

There is, in fact, only one ground on which one can give the least plausibility to the claim that the new religion helped woman—it takes a very ignorant man to say, as the Bishop of London does, that Christianity was " her best friend "—and that is the plea that amongst the licentious pagans she had been no more than " the creature of man's lusts," and that in regenerating morals the Church won new respect for her. That plea is fantastically untrue. Every Christian preacher and writer of the period of transition—Ambrose, Chrysostom, Jerome, Augustine, Salvianus, etc.—gives us clearly to understand that there was no improvement of the general level of character. Even the gentle Lecky says (II, 7) that " the two centuries after Constantine are uniformly represented by the Fathers as a period of general and scandalous vice." Salvianus (*De Gubernatione Dei*), who surveyed the

Christian world when the change of religion was complete (about 450), emphatically and repeatedly says that there is no improvement but some degeneration. And the next picture we have, Gregory of Tours's *History of Gaul* in the sixth century, is as revolting a calendar of vice and violence as one can imagine. After that, as we shall see, all Europe sank into barbarism.

Let me give one illustration how the pious fiction is—sometimes innocently—sustained. Writers take certain letters of St. Jerome and from these derive a picture of a few—about a dozen in all—very devout and charitable ladies who were his pupils in Rome. Here, of course, is the new Christian womanhood. But in some of the very letters which he sends to these women Jerome describes the body of Roman Christians, men and women, priests and laity, as quite generally and remarkably corrupt. His letters insist so often on the comprehensive corruption of Christian Rome in the latter part of the fourth century—that is to say, immediately after the forcible conversion of the Romans—that you will not find a translation of them in the various English libraries of works of the Fathers. And there is ample confirmation. In a Latin petition (published in the Migne Collection) of two Roman priests to the Emperor in the year 366 it is related that in one of many struggles over the election of a Pope 160 corpses were left on the floor of a church. The sermons of Augustine in Africa and of Chrysostom at Antioch and Constantinople reflect the same low general character. Chrysostom, the greatest Christian orator, complains that the people

will not come to hear him preach on sexual morals :
that their sins are " more numerous and more hein-
ous " than those of the pagans ; and even, referring
to the ancient Sodomites, that " now ten thousand
sins equal to and even more grievous than those are
committed."

There is, then, neither in the contemporary Christian
writers nor in modern historians the least justification
of the claim that morals improved when paganism
was suppressed, yet no claim is more persistently made
by the apologists, none more widely believed, than
that through the regeneration of morals Christianity
secured, as Dr. Fairbairn says, " a new respect for
women." Pictures of vice in Roman life two and even
four centuries before the triumph of Christianity are
pressed upon the reader. Bits of anti-aristocratic
gossip in Juvenal about a class and age to which he
did not belong are, against the warning of all authorities, given as history, and no one reproduces Sir
Samuel Dill's assurance that " in his [Juvenal's] own
class female morality was probably as high as the
average morality of any age " (*Roman Society from
Nero to Marcus Aurelius*, p. 76), or the even more
weighty verdict of Friedlaender, another Protestant :

There is nothing to show that in Imperial Rome shameless-
ness ever went so far as it did in Paris about the middle of
the eighteenth century (*Darstellungen aus der Sittengeschichte
Roms*, I, 431).

But I have given the full evidence in my *History of
Morals* and *History of the Roman Church* and cannot
enlarge here.

There was no change in the position, socially or

legally, of woman when Europe became Christian. No attempt has been made to produce one scrap of positive evidence of such a change. If there were any change, it ought to be for the worse, for the Fathers had almost uniformly used very dark language about woman as the cause of sin and of the curse of the race. But the robust women of the new Teutonic nations would not suffer it, and strange types of womanhood —the fierce Gallic princesses of the sixth century, the licentious noble women of Papal Rome in the tenth, the aggressive women of the courts of love and chivalry—continued for centuries to hold hectic and commanding positions in history. It was only when the spirit of the Fathers prevailed, when, from the eleventh century onward, a reformed Papacy got control of life, that woman, as we shall see, sank into the position of subjection and humiliation from which she has only recently been rescued by a less religious generation.

CHAPTER IV

THE SERFS OF THE DARK AGE

ONE is suspected by some of unscholarly partiality, of ponderous prejudice or, in the modern jargon, stubborn complexes, when in chapter after chapter one proves that the claim of the apologists is entirely unsound. But it is surely not impossible that these critics are themselves under the influence, if not of the apologetic literature itself, at least of the kind of literature which lazily and uncritically repeats the convention that somehow Christianity is in large part responsible for the unique progress of the Christian or white nations. This convention was rarely critically examined by the older historians, and more recent historians either confine themselves within such narrow limits of research that their opinion on the broad issue is worthless or do not find it prudent to affront the tradition. But the pressure of a sceptical age has compelled the theologians themselves to develop enormously that branch of their science which they call apologetics, and one of the primary tasks of this is to show from the historical facts that Christianity did actually help in the creation of Western civilization.

It is one of the most confused, most slovenly, and most reckless branches of literature. It has been one of my more painful duties to read every such work of importance that has appeared in half-a-dozen languages during the last fifty years, and no one who has this broad acquaintance with the literature can do other than pronounce it entirely bankrupt. I will give here one illustration. Probably the ablest and certainly one of the most honourable of such apologetic writers is Canon Streeter. In *The Spirit* (p. 358) he says :

The greatest blot on the history of the Church in modern times is the fact that, with the glaring exception of the campaign to abolish slavery, the leaders in the social, political, and humanitarian reforms of the last century and a half in Europe have rarely been professing Christians, while the authorized representatives of organized Christianity have, as often as not, been on the wrong side.

We shall see later the historical fallacy on the ground of which Canon Streeter claims for the Church a share in the abolition of black slavery; but listen to the words about it of an equally distinguished American apologist, Loring Brace (*Gesta Christi*) :

The guilt of this great crime rests upon the Christian Church as an organized body (p. 365).

He says expressly that " the very worst sin of the Churches is not helping abolition," and he then restores the credit of Christianity by claiming just those services which Canon Streeter comprehensively rejects. And on top of all this confusion, as if he had never heard of it and never read the serious literature of social history, the very latest apologist, Dr. A. W. Harrison, one of the leading

Nonconformist divines, says (*All That Jesus Began*, 1934, p. 53):

> From the Churches came the early leaders in the trade union movement and the co-operative societies: from them also came the inspiring challenge of the Christian Socialists and *the bulk of the men of strong character and personality who led in the high road of reform.*

And this is the last word in apologetics, written by the head of one of the chief colleges for training ministers, published by a body which claims to have 300,000 university students as members!

Since Dr. Harrison gives more space to slavery than to any other issue, those who suspect me of ignoring what is sound in the Christian claim will care to know what facts he opposes to those I have given. Let me premise that there is a peculiar difficulty. Dr. Harrison makes statements which flatly contradict those I have quoted from the leading experts, but he never gives exact references to any authorities. He quotes Lecky copiously, omitting what does not harmonize with his statements, and other writers, but never gives the reference: a singular proceeding in a book which is, it seems, intended for university students. We are told, for instance, that " it is in connection with the Church that we find the first traces of elementary schools." We learn that Christianity first built orphan asylums and " created hospitals." He tells us that " the last gladiatorial show " was held in 404, that the Telemachus story is sound, and that " a new standard of purity " and a great improvement in sex-morals came in the fourth century and elevated woman.

And for all these surprising revivals of legends which were, we thought, discredited decades ago we are not offered the least authority or testimony of facts.

However, let us get back to slavery and serfdom. Dr. Harrison assures us that the new Christian teaching was " a death-blow to slavery." Since he himself tells that it lingered in Christian Europe until the thirteenth century and began again in the sixteenth— I will show that it was really continuous to the nineteenth century—we feel that " death-blow " is not a happy expression. " Slavery," he says, " can never thrive side by side with real Christianity." It seems to have thriven remarkably both in Catholic and Protestant lands until the sceptics of the eighteenth century began the agitation for its suppression. But let us take the positive points of the matter.

Did Jesus or the Church condemn slavery ? No, he says, they were too wise to make a " frontal attack " on it, as this " might have done more harm than good." He does not say a word about Dio Chrysostom, Ulpian, and other Stoics who did condemn it. Next, who alleviated the lot of the slave ? He packs the long series of pagan enactments which I gave into a curt admission that " the humaner elements in stoicism [presumably Stoicism] had some influence in improving the lot of the slave " ; then he, without giving particulars or authority, surprisingly charges Trajan with " making their lot harder "—in the best of the Stoic days. But it was the Christian emperors who " steadily improved the lot of the slave by legislation "—he does not give a single law that I have

not given—and at last a great Christian leader in the
ninth century, Theodore of Stude, forbade Christians
to hold slaves. You may not have heard of this
philanthropist or even of Stude (which never existed).
Theodore was the Abbot of the Studium monastery
at Constantinople and had as much interest in social
questions as Simeon Stylites. What he really said
about slaves I cannot say, as no reference is given,
and the index to his weird works does not mention
them. Dr. Harrison has the grace to refrain from
claiming that this abolished or materially checked
slavery, but he says that by the twelfth century it
was rare and in the fourteenth it had " almost disappeared." The truth is that Venice and other Christian cities were very industrious in the slave-trade
until the fifteenth century. They then ceased, not
from religious reasons, but because the Turks ruined
their Greek customers in the East, and the Spaniards
destroyed their Moorish customers in Spain ; and the
Portuguese and Spaniards at once took their place in
the trade by beginning to kidnap Africans.

In short, this latest apologetic effort merely shows
how the fiction of Christian benevolence is maintained.
The book does not give the reader the least idea how
slavery was deeply modified and very greatly reduced
in pagan days : it exaggerates the very slender further
reforms of the Christian emperors : it keeps entirely
out of sight the enormous effect upon slavery of the
ruin of the Empire and its capitalists : and, above all,
it does not say a word about serfdom, and leaves the
inexpert reader imagining that, apart from a few tens
of thousands of slaves, the workers of Europe were

now free.   Serfdom is the next stage in the evolution
of the workers, and the guilt of the Church in regard
to it is so grave that one does not wonder that it is
not impressed upon the reader.   But first let us finish
with slavery, as few realize that it was *never* abolished
until the wicked French revolutionaries suppressed it
in all lands under their flag, and other nations were
inspired to follow.

Lecky had not at his command the facts about later
medieval slavery that we now have, but he says in his
History of European Morals (II, 30) :

Slavery lasted in Europe for about 800 years after Constantine, and during the period with which alone this volume
is concerned . . . the number of men who were subject to it
was probably greater than in the pagan Empire.

Lecky here either takes serfs and slaves together or he
forgets that the Slav and Teutonic nations which
had supplied the vast armies of Roman slaves were
now themselves, for the most part, masters and slave-
owners.   There was bound to be a drastic reduction
in the number of slaves.   But, in spite of the manumissions of which the chroniclers boast, and although
the new masters, whether nobles, bishops, or monasteries, had an equally profitable means of exploiting
the workers in serfdom, there were still large bodies
of slaves in the strict legal sense—men, women and
children who were the absolute property or chattels
of their owners.   It will be enough to give the facts
for England.

It is one of the purple patches of apologetic literature that the eleventh-century Bishop of Worcester,

St. Wulfstan, suppressed slavery in this country.   As the facts were given at length in Freeman's *Norman Conquest* sixty years ago, there is no excuse for the current and scandalous misrepresentation of them. Vinogradov estimates in his *Growth of the Manor* that there were 25,000 slaves in England when Domesday Book was compiled, or about the end of the eleventh century, and there were probably more at an earlier date.   Apart from Welsh captives, these were all English Christians who had been enslaved for crime or had sold themselves or been sold by parents in the periodical famines, when they were even known to eat human bodies.   These slaves were exported by the merchants of Bristol and other towns to Ireland, where they were resold to Danish shippers.   Traill's *Social England*, a generally reliable work, even says that this was " the chief trade of all " in the England of the eleventh century (I, 296).   The Churchmen, who had not the least mind to " break the fetters of the slave " in England, were indignant that they should be shipped to lands where they might have heathen masters, and all that Wulfstan did was to protest against this foreign traffic.   Æthelred had forbidden it seventy years earlier, and Cnut had renewed the law.   It was disregarded, and Wulfstan spent months in Bristol threatening the traders with hell.   But it is untrue that he suppressed even the foreign trade.   His Latin biographer, quoted in Freeman (IV, 386), merely says that the merchants dropped the trade " for a time," and years later we find the bishops still complaining of it.

" What the preaching of Wulstan and Anselm, the legislation of Cnut and William, failed to do " was, says Freeman, accomplished by " the oligarchic contempt of the lower classes " of their new Norman masters.   They abolished slavery, but they got rid of the distinction between serf and slave by so lowering the condition of the serf or villain that Freeman calls it " the blackest and saddest result of the Norman Conquest."   We shall see their condition presently. Meantime, the causes of slavery of the old Roman days were still operative all over Christendom.   North and west of the Christian nations were uncivilized and pagan peoples, and, though they could not furnish the masses of war-captives which the Roman armies had made, they in each century provided fresh supplies. Men were also enslaved for crime, were kidnapped, and sold themselves or their children.   An even more repulsive traffic was maintained by France and Italy than the Bristol slave-trade ;   though the English chronicles tell us how the English traders used to make their young-women slaves pregnant and then demand a higher price for them.

S. P. Scott says, in his *Moorish Empire in Europe*, that in the ninth and tenth centuries the monks of Verdun, far away in the north of France, did a prosperous trade in buying sons of the peasants of the region, castrating and rearing them, and selling them as eunuch-slaves to the Moors and the Greeks (through Venice).   Familiar as I was with the barbarities of the Middle Ages, I found this incredible, and I made some research into the matter.   It transpired that Bishop Liutprand, one of the best writers of the time, tells us (*Antapodosis*, VI, 6) that Verdun, a town which was controlled by its bishop, *was* a notorious centre of this loathsome industry ; and, in view of the grossness of the time and the power of bishops, it seems probable that the monasteries there and in other parts of France were so engaged. The Spanish Christians, I found, used to make the Moorish Caliph presents of eunuch-slaves of this type. So slavery was maintained all over Europe, and most of all in that half of Christendom, the Greek half, which the barbarians had never entered.

Serfdom had by this time become just as profitable to the masters, and slavery shrank as the pagan areas for recruiting slaves shrank and the price rose. But it is, as I said, entirely wrong to suppose that slavery was suppressed in Europe and after a long interval restored for the American market. The Venetians were still selling slaves when the advance of the Turks ruined their Greek trade, but just at the same period, the middle of the fifteenth century, the Arabs were driven out of Spain and Portugal, and the Portuguese took over the Arab shipping and at once began raids in Africa, while the Spaniards raided what is now Algeria and Tunisia. Dr. Agate says, in the *Encyclopædia of Religion and Ethics*, that instead of a break between an older system of slavery and the enslaving of the Africans, to which we will return in the sixth chapter, we have " one of the most remarkable and deplorable instances of historical continuity." It is remarkable only to those who are persuaded that the spread of Christianity was " a death-blow " to slavery. All that happened was that the triumph of the Turks destroyed the oriental trade and shipping of the Italians and stimulated the Spanish, Portuguese, French, and English to take them over. They were not forbidden by their religion to enslave, and the discovery of America gave a portentous new development to the trade.

We to-day interpret on similar economic lines what happened in Europe itself. We may fully recognize all the acts of Christian piety which took the form of manumitting slaves, but these had a small part in the transformation. It had begun in pagan days. The supply of agricultural slaves, we saw, diminished, and, besides the free farmers, a new type, the *colonus*, tied to the soil but not the property of any other man, appeared. Others, " quasi-colonists," had even less freedom. Then came the ruin of the great estates and their owners, and, in the general desolation, the ex-slaves and peasants would come to offer their services to new masters. The great majority became " serfs," which is a French form of the Latin word for slaves.

It is an extremely complicated development and must be read in technical treatises, but the summary of it is that, while there were more free men than slaves in the fourth century, *the great majority* of the workers after the fifth century sank to a condition that differs in little more than technical definition from that of the slave. The formal difference is that the slave is owned by the master just in the same sense as his horse or his dog, while the serf, though not personally owned, is tied to the soil which the master owns, can be sold with it, and is compelled to give a

considerable part of his labour to the land-owner.
But there were, as Vinogradov shows in his various
works on English life, very many variations of the
serf's position, or of the position of the agricultural
worker in general, and some of these were indistinguish- ..
able from slavery. In *Villainage in England* he
shows that in the thirteenth century—the ideal century of Catholic apologists—the majority of English
peasants were villains (the English equivalent of serfs),
and that in law they were not tied to the soil but
were the personal property of the lords and abbots, and
subject to them.   The State took no interest in them
and excluded them from its courts, so that they were
wholly destitute of the protection which the pagan
emperors had given to the Roman slave.   The distinction between serf and slave in its application to
the majority of English workers—in *English Society
in the Eleventh Century* he shows that the villains alone
represent 100,000 out of 240,000 households in Domesday Book ; Traill describes them as " the great bulk of
the population "—is, Vinogradov concludes, "late and
artificial."

This was the condition of England and, with very
considerable local variations, of all Christendom from
the seventh to the thirteenth century, and of large areas
of Europe to the eighteenth or nineteenth century :
an ironic comment on " the brotherhood of man "
and " the abolition of slavery."   The Catholic historian Guizot said that in the eighth and ninth centuries the Church was " a population of slaves " ;
though he need not have confined his description to
two centuries.   They worked from sunrise to sunset

on, Thorold Rogers shows, 300 days of the 365. Their homes were one-room earth-floored hovels, in which man, wife, and children lived and slept like pigs. Their sexual practices, as shown in the lists of sins given in such contemporary documents as the *Ecclesiastical Discipline* of Abbot Regino of Prum, would have made an ancient Roman worker raise his eyebrows. They had no redress against the officials of the land-owner except in his (or their) own court. One often finds it repeated that Schmidt has shown in his *Jus primae noctis* that it is a libel that the lords claimed the peasant bride's first night. On the contrary, the evidence in Schmidt's book shows that such a claim was common. But there was, in any case, no need to invoke legal rights against a serf. Bede tells us that in Anglo-Saxon England it was " the inveterate custom " for the noble to appropriate any handsome young woman and " sell her when she became pregnant." In many places, however, including England, the lord, even if an abbot or bishop, had the legal right to the first night, and as late as the fifteenth century we find French peasants complaining of it.

For such complaints in the Dark Age they would have been brutally flogged or have had their noses or ears cut off. The punishments and mutilations of the serfs were appalling. In 997 the serfs of Count Raoul of Evreux were stung into revolt by his cruelty. He hamstrung all of them, impaled or burned or poured boiling lead over some, and cut out the eyes or broke out the teeth of others. A German noble had forbidden a peasant girl to marry, but she mar-

C

ried, and she and her man fled to the altar. The noble promised that he would " not separate them," and when they came out of the church, he had the young pair tied breast to breast and buried alive. An Italian noble took a servant who had spilled soup over him in his own arms and put him on the huge fire in the hall. Few in those days were the Abbot Samp-sons, sons of the people themselves, who held courts where even a serf could ask justice. The atmosphere was so sodden with barbaric violence that in the con-fessional-books we find the priest directed to ask peni-tents, as a matter of course : Have you cut out any man's eyes or cut off his nose, ears, or testicles ? In law boiling oil and molten lead were used, weights hung from the sex-organ, eyes, ears, tongues and noses cut off, water dropped from a height upon the stomach, etc.

This side of medieval life comes under proper con-sideration in any inquiry into the social record of Christianity, but a few generalizations would be un-convincing, and for details I should require a large volume. I have packed two books (V and VIII) of my *History of Morals* and several books of my *True Story of the Roman Catholic Church* with such details taken from contemporary chronicles. Here let us finish with serfdom.

We will suppose that generally the serfs of the abbeys had better conditions, but, on the other hand, the clergy and monks were the last to give freedom. Their serfs were, the clerics said, " Church-property " and must not be " alienated." It was, again, econo-mic causes that in the thirteenth and fourteenth centuries destroyed serfdom over the greater part of Europe. Nobles wanted money to equip themselves for the Crusades, and they sold their " freedom "— we shall see what it was worth—to tens of thousands of serfs. Kings wanted their co-operation against nobles or nobles against kings, or one city against another. Many found, as Roman land-owners had done, that a free and willing worker was more valuable than a serf. So the great body bought emancipation, by money or services, and the religious manumissions, however admirable, counted for little.

But there was no condemnation by any Church, Roman, Greek, or (from the sixteenth century) Protestant. Very large bodies of serfs remained in every country. In France there were tens of thousands down to the outbreak of the Revolution. In England there were serfs until the sixteenth century ; in Germany and Austria until the eighteenth ; in Russia 42,500,000 serfs had to be emancipated (and pay for it themselves) under the pressure of liberalism in the year 1861. It was, however, mainly over, apart from Russia, by the end of the fourteenth century. The industrial and civic development aided the other causes I have indicated. Until the twelfth century there was little trade or money in Europe, and industrial workers were relatively few. It was an age of home industries, very small towns, and sordid poverty. In the twelfth century began the multiplication and growth of free towns, the accumulation of wealth, the development of large bodies of craftsmen. But the low condition in which the workers still were only a hundred years ago ought to warn any man that behind all the artistic blaze of the later Middle Ages the workers still led a life which was that of a slave in comparison with the life of the old free workers of Rome or Greece.

CHAPTER V

THE AGE OF GUILDS AND CHIVALRY

ROUGHLY, and if one does not take the figures as other than round numbers, we may divide the history of Europe since the beginning of the Christian Era into four equal parts. During the first 500 years the older Greco-Roman civilization flourished and decayed. The next 1,000 years are the real Christian Era, the period when the Church was strong enough to silence or destroy its critics and wield such power, even over princes and scholars, as the world had never before witnessed. But this, the Middle Age—it is unfortunate that the phrase Middle Ages is so deeply rooted—is very properly divided into two parts, the first half (really, from about 500 to 1050) being most justly called the Dark Age, the second half being the Age of Recovery or the Dawn Age. From 1500 to 2000 will probably be known in time as the Age of Struggle, when (as in *Chanticleer*, which is a deliberate symbol of it) the creatures of the night made their last long and bloody fight against the light.

I pass over with disdain a few recent attempts of third-rate historical writers to prove that there never was a Dark Age. They prove only that some scholar or saint or good man here and there in the vast dark wilderness, kept his little lamp burning for a time. It is more important to understand that life was still half-barbaric from 1000 to 1500, and long afterwards.   The entire period which I call the real Christian Era (500–1500), because then only had the Church full power, is the longest and worst reaction that has broken the onward march of the race since the dawn of civilization.   I have been compelled at times to regret passages in Lecky's *History of European Morals* which, severed from the context, are used in the service of reaction.   But let me quote summary passages from the beginning of his second volume, when he sets out to survey the new Christian world :

> Few persons, I think, who had contemplated Christianity as it existed in the first three centuries would have imagined it possible that it should completely supersede the pagan worship around it ; that its teachers should bend the mightiest monarchs to their will and stamp their influence on every page of legislation, and direct the whole course of civilization for a thousand years ; and yet that the period in which they were so supreme should have been *one of the most contemptible in history* (p. 6).
>
> The ecclesiastical civilization which followed [A.D. 550 to 1550], though not without its distinctive merits, assuredly supplies no justification of the common boast about the regeneration of society by the Church (p. 7).

Lecky also at least indicates the answer to the sophists who throw all the blame upon the barbaric invaders and claim that the condition of Europe prevented Christianity from having a fair trial ; and, further to redeem his memory, I give it in his own fine words :

> It is often said that . . . in judging the ignorance of the Dark Ages we must make allowance for the dislocations of society by the barbarians.   In all this there is much truth ;

but when we remember that in the Byzantine Empire the renovating power of theology was tried in a new capital free from pagan traditions, and for more than one thousand years unsubdued by barbarians, and that in the West the Church, for at least seven hundred years after the shocks of the invasions had subsided, exercised a control more absolute than any other moral or intellectual agency has ever attained, it will appear, I think, that the experiment was very sufficiently tried (p. 7).

To this I need add only two observations. The Byzantine or Greek half of Christendom was not merely " unsubdued by barbarians " but never seriously invaded, yet, as I show in my *Empresses of Constantinople*, it sank almost as speedily and almost as low as the Latin half from the Greco-Roman level, and its chronicles are full of sordid vices, murderous greeds, and savage mutilations.

The next matter, which Lecky's studies did not give him occasion to appreciate, is that in point of historical fact such efforts as were made in Europe to prevent it from sinking into barbarism or to restore it to civilization were all due to the Teutonic invaders and were hampered, and often wrecked, by the Church. I should be the last to defend Hitlerism, but when its English critics issued a pamphlet and invited Mr. G. K. Chesterton to claim in a preface that the Teutonic elements contributed only barbarism to European life and Rome was the angel of light, I willingly replied to him (*Mr. G. K. Chesterton as an Historical Oracle*). In undisputed history four attempts were made during the Dark Age to restore civilization. In the first half of the sixth century Theodoric the Goth and his accomplished daughter Amalasuntha made a noble effort, of which fine monuments survive at Ravenna ; and the Papacy and the Greeks wrecked it.   In the eighth century the Lombards from the north settled in the area that the Goths had civilized, and again made it the most advanced part of Europe ; and the Papacy got the Franks to wreck their work.   Charlemagne, who completed this ruin for the Pope, was nevertheless stimulated by Lombard culture to make a fresh attempt, and his work was defeated by his clergy, in alliance with a (in his later years) hostile Papacy.   And the fourth and, in so far as it started the great architectural movement, most successful was that of the German Emperor Otto I in the tenth century.

It is a notorious fact that this fourth attempt of Teutonic princes to restore civilization coincided with the hundred years of appalling degradation at Rome which the older Catholic historians bluntly called " The Rule of the Whores."   Instead of Rome assisting the revival, it was so sodden with vice and ignorance, that the German emperors had to chasten it with the flat of the sword, which took many decades, and it was Teutonic Popes like Hildebrand who reformed it.   Unfortunately, they went to the opposite extreme. They were ferocious puritans and sacerdotalists, deadly enemies of all lay culture and liberty, ready at all times to use every weapon, from forgery to bloodshed, to promote their aims.   It was they who brought to Italy the last fierce (and most vicious) invaders from the North, the Normans, but, though for a time the Normans brutally ravaged Italy, they within a few generations gave it the greatest constructive monarch of the Middle Ages, Frederic II, " the Wonder of the World."

Why were the Normans, who were as fierce as and in their vices more lawless than any other Northern peoples, civilized in a century, if we are to believe that Europe was kept in semi-barbarism for a thousand years because of its invaders ? This small manual is just a summary of criticisms of Christian claims and cannot enlarge upon the real constructive forces of European civilization. I must be content to say that immeasurably the strongest stimulation that began to awaken Christendom from its medieval nightmare came from the brilliant civilization which liberal Arabs and Persians had now created in Spain, Sicily, and the east. It was because the Normans settled in Sicily that they were civilized so rapidly ; it was because the Albigensians, or the people of the south of France, were the nearest neighbours of the Arabs of Spain that they rose to a high civilization. The full truth about the reawakening of Europe at this stage is so fatal to the legend of Christian inspiration that history is only now daring to tell it. When, for instance, Lord Acton planned the great Cambridge Medieval History, only about 50 pages out of 5,000 were allotted to the fine civilizations of Moorish Spain and Saracen Sicily—which had four times the population and a hundred times the wealth and culture of the Christian part of Europe—and, apparently, no English historian could be found to write them.

The reader will care to know that the Rationalist Press Association will shortly publish for me an adequate account of this fine civilization and its influence upon Europe. Here one word must suffice. It is that the story of the Arab civilization makes a mockery of the claim, in which too many historians had idly acquiesced, that the barbaric invaders of Europe could not have been civilized by any agency in less than a thousand years. The men who poured out from the Arabian deserts in the seventh century were even more barbaric, more savage in war and as unbridled in vice, as the Teutons and Normans. Yet within two generations they founded a high civilization in Syria, and by the tenth century, the Iron Age of Christendom, it deployed its vast wealth, its culture, and its social idealism from Portugal to the confines of India. How this taught Europe, through Spain, Sicily, and the Crusades, to be ashamed of its boorishness I must tell elsewhere.

Coinciding with this tuition there was, of course, a native economic development in Christendom. How far the creation of a high civilization in Spain, which preceded the European economic development by two centuries, influenced even this it would be difficult to estimate. But a body of ten million people, living amidst memorials of an earlier civilization, cannot remain indefinitely in squalid poverty, and, especially after the Saxon revival under Otto I and his successors, a modest prosperity slowly spread. It still took, as we saw, two centuries for this to affect the great mass of the people and liberate the serfs in large numbers. However, especially in Germany and North Italy, towns grew, wealth and trade increased, and the demand naturally arose for art and civic self-government, and presently for education.

The guilds of the town-workers, which now became a picturesque feature of city life, had begun much earlier and had an interesting origin. They appear first in the laws (Capitularies) of Charlemagne, and they appear only to be drastically condemned. Although writers on the guilds do not care to admit it, since Christian apologists are now very eager to claim the glory of the guilds for the Church, the only plausible explanation of their origin is that they were revivals of the old unions or " colleges " of Greek and Roman workers, the ghosts of which still lingered in Rome and Constantinople. Dr. Gross (*The Gild-Merchant*) will not admit this, yet he says that " the Church fostered the early growth of the gilds and tried to make them displace the old heathen banquets." What were these old heathen banquets in the ninth century, the earliest date at which the Church patronized the guilds ? From the words of the imperial and ecclesiastical decrees it is quite clear. From the year 779, when the people are sternly forbidden to " conspire together in guilds " (V, 16), to the year 852, when an ecclesiastical synod at Nantes condemns the banquets of these guilds—incidentally admitting that the priests get drunk and sing ribald songs at them—we see the Church drastically condemning and trying to suppress the guilds.

Thus, instead of " fostering the early guilds," the Church—I am quoting direct from the Capitularies and synodal decrees—recognizing the pagan features that clung to them, was bitterly opposed. At last it had to permit them on condition that they were put under the direction of the clergy. It is unfortunate that the leading writers on the guilds, whom our encyclopædias follow, never examined this earlier evidence. The development was familiar enough. What the Church could not suppress it captured and consecrated, in its own interest. Then, when the rapid industrial expansion occurred in the thirteenth century, the large guilds of the workers became very conspicuous and for a time useful features of town life. But the writers on them are agreed that within a century or two they became mischievous. They ruined towns by their conservatism and exactions. They died a natural death in the fifteenth and sixteenth centuries.

Meantime at the other end of the social scale, amongst the nobility, there occurred a development about which all apologists used to write with pride, as the more innocent apologists still do. This is seen in the troubadours on the one hand and the knights on the other, though we may take them together as the age of chivalry. The most flourishing period of this is from about 1100 to about 1300. In other words, it begins just after the reform of the Church by Hildebrand, the imposition of celibacy on the clergy, and the increasing control of life by them ; and it coincides with the great age of cathedral-building, the period of the Crusades, and the busy life of the early medieval universities. But recent literary and historical experts are generally agreed that it was a free-love movement of the most defiant character, in which the women were to a surprising extent more aggressive than the men. Unfortunately, this recent study has been done chiefly in French and German works, but the best English authority, J. F. Rowbotham (*The Troubadours and Courts of Love*), says :

Immorality was fostered *as it has rarely been before or since* by this exceeding freedom of intercourse, which at any time might bring a fascinating and brilliant stranger into the midst of a family circle and give him the privilege of access and intimate communication with every member of it.

My friend, Mr. George Moore, who detested research at the Museum, at one time got me to read for him several volumes of French troubadour poetry. I found the freedom amazing. The women, married and single, in particular, are so forward that even that eminent sexologist, Mr. Havelock Ellis, is misled into speculating that the exacting labours of the knights left them tired and reluctant. The plain reading of the literature is, as Krabbes and all other experts point out, that just in this age of cathedral-building and Crusades the women of the aristocracy, of the court of love and the field of tournament, quite generally ignored the sex-ethic.

The conventional belief in the " honour " of the knights is as little justified by the literature of the period as is the belief in the " virtue " of their ladies. Tennyson's *Idylls* is just an idealization of the later and expurgated literature of chivalry. Religious knights and troubadours and virtuous ladies there certainly were, but the extensive study of the whole period in recent decades, especially of the earlier literature, has shown that the ladies were generally immoral and the knights generally boorish, vicious, and unjust. Traill's *Social England* long ago pointed out that the knights, whom so many people (including novelists and painters) imagine sallying forth daily to aid some damsel in distress, used, on the contrary, to violate any unprotected woman they met and robbed even the poor. The monks of Peterborough, who continue the English Chronicle, give this general description of the Norman knights after the Conquest :

> They took all those that they deemed had any goods, men and women, and tortured them with tortures unspeakable ; never were martyrs so tortured as they were. Many thousands they slew with hunger . . . they robbed and burned all the villages.

And William of Malmesbury (*History of Recent Events*, II, 30, 36) tells us how they tortured women, priests, and monks to make them tell where they had hidden their money. Monks were burned alive in their monasteries. Men were smeared with honey, naked, and pegged out in the sun to attract insects. Add that these Norman knights of the cathedral-building age were more addicted to unnatural vice than Romans or Greeks had ever been, and you may have a new idea of the ages of faith.

This troubadour age and age of chivalry, beginning in northern Spain, the south of France (from which our lively Queen Eleanor came), and North Italy was —though I must admit that a few dispute this— directly inspired by the Moors and Saracens ; while amongst these there was at least great refinement, and the tournaments were bloodless. Not in Arabic literature would you find a princess, as I found one in a French troubadour song, urging her knights to " hit the enemy in the guts and then choose amongst the most beautiful ladies of the court." But, as I said, the question of medieval morals is too vast to be treated here. I want to make two points clear. One is that the idea that the building of the cathedrals implies an improvement of morals and piety in Europe is very far astray. The romantically inclined ought to read a candid description of the very gross and obscene Feast of Fools, Feast of the Ass, etc., which the bishops and clergy permitted in the very sanctuaries and at the altars of the cathedrals. The second and, for my present purpose, more important point is that the troubadour movement, borrowed from the Arabs, was the chief source of the new literary and artistic life of Europe. It seized all classes. The great scholar Abelard was before his tragic experience just as distinguished for song and music as for learning. The monasteries and convents resounded with gay melody. Thus were the vernacular languages of Europe slowly forged and prepared for the use of a Dante and a Chaucer. . . . It had been nearly nine centuries since Europe had produced a book, Augustine's *City of God*, which anybody but a literary expert reads to-day.

It was a marvellous, a tantalizing and almost indescribable, world. Many years ago I gave a comprehensive picture of it in my *Peter Abelard*. On one side were the thousands of students pressing along every road, the fiery preaching of Bernard and his monks, the rich atmosphere of cathedrals : on the other hand the unbridled license of people, priests, nuns, and monks, a canon hiring men to castrate Abelard, the great scholar appealing to the law to punish the canon in the same way, monks poisoning the wine of Abelard's chalice and lying in wait for their abbot with knives. Heloise, now a mother-superior, boasting of her monk-lover's embraces in her convent-chapel . . . Civilization, yes, but more than streaked with barbarism.   The law was gross in its procedure, filthy and brutal as an ancient Chinese court in its punishments. City streets were as foul as those of villages, and epidemics mowed down millions.   The Black Death killed 25,000,000 and racked the whole population.   Murderous bandits infested every road.   This age of artistic splendour, of crusades (chiefly for loot, as we now perceive), of saints, of superb churches, of anathemas and interdicts, was, says even the Positivist historian Cotter Morison, " an age of violence, fraud, and impurity such as can hardly be conceived now."   Such is the verdict wrung from the admiring biographer of Bernard of Clairvaux, when he turns to a general study of the age.

CHAPTER VI

THE PEOPLE IN THE AGE OF BEAUTY

CAN we find no services of the Church or of the Christian religion in this flowering of European life in the twelfth, thirteenth, and fourteenth centuries ? Of course we can. It goes without saying that in many places there were devout bishops, abbots, or abbesses who worked for justice and peace : that the new ferment of school-life helped to awaken the slumbering mind of Europe : that the rich artistic development helped to refine and gladden life, and the Church was at first the chief patron of art. But if we wish to have a serious and true conception of what social service Christianity rendered and might further render we have, surely, to be clear in our minds on two points. First, we not only fool ourselves but encourage others to continue in deceit unless we resolutely discredit false claims. Next, we must obviously distinguish between services rendered by men who were Christians and services rendered by them solely because they were Christians.

In regard to the first point I submit that the preceding five chapters have annihilated all claims of social service of Christianity to this date, or, say, to A.D. 1100. It is a quite graceful task to search the arid chronicles of those centuries for an abbot here and there who opened a school or protected the poor, a saint who rebuked violence and injustice, and so on. But that is not history and it usually does more harm than good. Our literature is still steeped with the spurious claims of apologists, and we have to insist on broad truths and general conditions. On the balance of good and evil, the Christian religion plainly hindered the restoration of civilization in Europe. You cannot even say that it was the so-called Christians, not Christianity, who did this, for the more profoundly religious Popes, prelates, and abbots were, the more they despised culture, art (as such), social and political ethics, and all purely secular interests. No men did more at this time to check the restoration of civilization than Bernard, Hildebrand, and Innocent III, the three supreme religious figures of the age.

These men despised the artistic movement and sought to sterilize the intellectual movement, and these were the two most promising aspirations of the new mind of Europe. They are, in fact, almost the only new development we need consider. There was no material change in the brutality of law, though the ordeal was suppressed. There was not only no improvement in, but a very profound deterioration of, the position of woman, especially after the abolition of divorce. There was no new conception of humanity, for violence, mutilations, duels and local wars, delight in animal-fights, and the exploitation of the weak were as blatant as ever. Cruelty in Renaissance days often took on the form of fiendishness ; and unquestionably the Christian doctrine of the vindictiveness of God and the new bloody zeal of the Church against heretics encouraged this.

As to the intellectual or scholastic life, it was at first a very modest ecclesiastical advance. Bishops and abbots decided to open schools for the training of the clergy, as old law bade them. There was a very rapid expansion of this when independent and largely sceptical and brilliant men like Abelard set up as teachers; when (simultaneously) news and specimens of Moorish culture spread over Europe; when (again simultaneously) the troubadour movement stimulated minds and the growing wealth and commerce set free thousands of youths to wander in search of excitement in the cities and their schools. It was all part of the new life of Europe, an outcome of the new blood that pulsed in its veins. No impulse from the Church was needed or was given, but within a single generation the Church began to check it and try to confine it to the respectful and entirely orthodox discussion of religious themes.

The ages of faith, if we give that name specifically to the twelfth and thirteenth centuries—and the faith of the profoundly ignorant centuries that had preceded is hardly a thing of which one may boast—were also the first great ages of heresy and revolt. While Abelard gave the signal of intellectual revolt, his pupil, Arnold of Brescia, raised again the claim of democracy. Both were crushed by the Church, but the Papacy had to fight for a hundred years the democratic claims of the Romans themselves, and the revolt against Papal authority was never silenced. The myth of the docility of the Middle Ages is one of the most astonishing survivals in our literature.   Revolt began at once with the awakening, and in three centuries more than a million rebels against the Church (Albigensians, Cathari, Lollards, and Hussites, besides the victims of the Inquisition and of the courts that preceded it) were savagely put to death ; if we include witches (whom we now know to have been an anti-clerical organization of people of both sexes and all ages and conditions), there were probably several million victims before the Reformation occurred. From the twelfth century onward thinking Europe was bludgeoned into docility, and its new culture was sterilized.   The zeal for science, which Roger Bacon and others learned from the Moors—there is not a word in Bacon's works that is not Moorish science— was extinguished.   Philosophy was enslaved and made " the hand-maid of theology."   The crowds that filled the universities of the thirteenth and fourteenth centuries, the numbers of which have been grossly exaggerated, were almost entirely priestlings and monklings learning medieval theology.

I have here to condense what I have shown at length, with full contemporary evidence, in my American works, and I must dismiss the subject of art even more curtly.   Art always advances with wealth, and the new wealth of Europe gathered most thickly in the coffers of priests and nobles.   The kings and nobles spent theirs in the adventure of the Crusades, in wars, in heavy castles that had to sustain sieges, and, when the Arabs taught them to wash themselves, in personal luxury and adornment.   The Church naturally spent much of its wealth on archi-

tecture and the ancillary arts ; for not a single not-
able church had been built in Europe for five or six
centuries, while travellers told of Arab mosques which
had cost, in our coinage, £60,000,000. In the thirteenth and fourteenth centuries, we saw, cities pur-
chased their charters of freedom and grew in wealth
and numbers, and it became a matter of civic pride
to have a church or cathedral which should be the
finest in the land.

By that time art had burst its clerical bonds and
was part of the spring-flush of the new Europe.
When the Church's *patronage* of art is perversely represented as a Christian *inspiration* of the great art of
the Middle Ages, we must ask the historian of art if
it would not have developed if there had been no
Christian Church. He smiles. It was as irrepres-
sible an outcome of the new wealth and awakening
as had been the art of Greece in the time of Pericles,
of that of China under the Tang emperors. So any
modern historian of art will tell you. The early evolution of the Gothic art of the great cathedrals is
obscure, though we do know that the monasteries of
central France which took the leading part were
generally frivolous and corrupt. But there is no
obscurity about the further development of medieval
art. To the middle of the thirteenth century, say
Woltmann and Woermann in their authoritative *History of Painting*, there were in Europe (and in the
hands of the monks) only " the painting and sculpture
of children." Then the arts " emancipated themselves from priestly dictation," and it was in the
period of the Renaissance, strictly conceived, the

fifteenth and early sixteenth centuries, the least Christian and most immoral period that Italy had yet known, that " the highest beauty, which the gods themselves had, two thousand years earlier, revealed to the Greeks, now revisited earth among the Italians." Rome, the heart of Christendom, did not even patronize art until this last period, when artists painted or carved Aphrodite as lovingly as St. Catherine, and a frivolous little sceptic like Pinturicchio could use the Pope's mistress, Giulia Orsini, as a model for his picture of the Virgin on a wall of the Vatican.

These matters I must notice briefly and return to the question of the condition of the mass of the people. I have said that the laws under which they lived remained barbarous. At the very height of Rome's culture, about the year 1500, you would find civic officials bearing on a pole through the streets, amidst ribald crowds, the organ of a man who had been condemned to castration. The political regime was worse than ever, as the kings crushed the nobles and exercised a despotic authority. Through the rejection of Moorish science, which had cleansed the great cities of Spain and greatly advanced medicine and surgery, Europe remained foul and suffering. And it was only after one of the periodical epidemics or a savage war or both had removed hundreds of thousands of workers that, owing to scarcity of labour, there was any improvement of their condition.

It is a common weakness of history that it usually describes the life and deeds of only a minority of a nation. It is the statesmen and churchmen, the nobles and artists, the generals and writers, who fill the chronicles. What reader of general history knows how nine people out of ten lived in Rome or Athens or Thebes? We begin, however, to feel that one of the most searching tests of a civilization is the condition of the mass of the people, which history has been wont to ignore, and social experts are bringing to light the misery that lay in the shadows of the great cathedrals and was scattered over the country. It must seem probable to any man who knows medieval life that the great majority of the population never saw a cathedral or any other work of art of the Middle Ages. How many of the hundreds of thousands living in the spacious country between London, Canterbury, Winchester, and Peterborough, in an age when the poor travelled afoot and never had more than a day's holiday, can ever have seen those shrines?

The misery of life is sufficiently reflected in the figures of population. During the second half of the Middle Ages, or from 1066 to 1500, the period of which the Catholic apologist is so proud, the population of this country, where people then bred like rabbits, just doubled; and it trebled during the nineteenth century alone, in spite of the ghastly industrial conditions of the first half and the practice of birth-control in the second half. The romantic idea of our medieval fathers dancing merrily on the green and quaffing real ale as they sat in clean smocks before the ale-house is as mythical as the snowy Christmas or the taller stature of early days. Life was for them, as in that ancient oriental vision, a bridge set with traps to the end of which few persevered. The average duration of life, which is now fifty years and is

steadily growing, was then, medical authorities estimate, about twenty years.

Let us realize that the overwhelming mass of the
people of Europe, outside Arab Spain, were still agricultural workers. Of the 2,500,000 people of England in the thirteenth century less than a tenth lived
in towns. These nine-tenths of the nation were now
" free " in the sense that they did not belong to a
master, but, as Thorold Rogers points out, they rarely
got away from a village of sixty to eighty people.
On six days a week, except on three holidays in the
year, they worked from sunrise to sunset, wresting
from the soil by the crudest methods the subsistence
of 30,000 priests and monks, the income of their
feudal lords, and the king's taxes. Of food, according to Professor Thorold Rogers, who says the best
one can truthfully say for these days, there was a
" coarse plenty " : a small range of vegetables, salt
meat (causing scurvy and leprosy everywhere) during
half the year, and a coarse bread—not wheaten—in
moderation. Even the nobles ate with their fingers
and rarely used plates.

The home was still a one-room hovel, generally
built of wattle daubed with mud, with an earth-floor
(never cleaned), no chimney, and no windows. Often
the pig and the few fowls shared it. Father, mother,
and children simply flung off their outer garments at
nightfall and lay together on the straw, as I have seen
Syrian gypsies do. Even in the castles and schools
straw covered the floor, and dogs fouled it—and, in
short, handkerchiefs were unknown. And at night,
when the gentry had gone to their chambers, some-

times six or more in a bed, sleeping in their sweaty woollen day-shirts, the retainers swept away the foul straw, and all ages and both sexes stripped to their shirts and dragged out their straw mattresses on the hall-floor. In a document of the time a lady forbids her servants to extinguish the candle with their (short) shirts to spare their fingers. Even in the inns travellers and pilgrims thus slept, in their day-shirts, without separation of sexes. Dufour reproduces in his *Histoire de la prostitution* a charter in which a noble French dame of the thirteenth century releases prostitutes who visit her small town to ply their trade from the customary tax (in coin or kind), on condition that each comes to the drawbridge of the castle and, doubtless to the great hilarity of all the men, women, and children of the town, raises her skirts and makes a very rude noise. These were the cathedral-builders.

But it is most improper to translate these Latin and early French documents for our generation, to let people see what manner of folk these really were who built the cathedrals ; and, indeed, if I begin to discuss the morals of these people we shall make no progress. All the beauty and glamour of the thirteenth and fourteenth centuries coincided with a grossness of taste and morals that is to us inconceivable. Let us return to the social aspect of the life of the people.

It need not be said that these ninety per cent of the people of Europe, the agricultural workers, were totally illiterate and of an incredible ignorance and superstition, which the clergy exploited. But the artisans of the towns, the members of the guilds, were in little better condition. They had no better food than the peasant, and they had the same maladies from so much salt meat and salt fish. The streets were almost as foul as the village streets: lakes of mud when it rained, stinking in summer from the garbage and domestic superfluities which everybody flung there. At Cnossos, in Crete, I saw an excellent drainage-system, with collar-headed pipes, in a palace which had been built 3,500 years ago. No European city (outside Spain and Sicily) had any sanitary system until long after the end of the Middle Ages. So pestilence swept repeatedly, and with deadly havoc, over Christendom, and men were driven into the insanities of dancing-manias, scourging-manias, and so on. In the towns was the added terror of the innumerable thieves and cut-throats. You locked up your daughter and your money very securely in that age of piety; and even this availed little when the soldiers were on campaign or a lord and his bullies prowled the streets at night. License to rape, loot, and kill was granted to every army which in those quarrelsome days hacked its way across Europe. And when men rebelled, as they did under Wat Tyler and John Ball, and the king's men made havoc of them, the Church bade them reconcile themselves to the position in which the Almighty had placed them. When the barons had checked the power of John, one of the most brutal of kings, the Pope declared their Magna Charta a " devil-inspired document."

In our history lessons we still tell children how our sturdy peasants bore themselves at Crécy and Agincourt. We might do better to tell them how this depletion of the country, to satisfy a stupid royal greed which the Church blessed, led repeatedly to famine, in which the people ate cats and dogs, and even human beings. There were times when the prisoners in jail were so starved that they murdered and ate new-comers. And Traill's *Social History* adds (it not being intended for children) :

> Whatever the common people suffered, the upper classes were living in luxury, and most of all the monks, who were at no period more splendid in their equipages and households.

Wyclif tells us that after the Black Death had carried off in terrible agony twenty thousand out of the forty thousand people of London, the friars would not visit the houses of the poorer survivors because of " the stink and other filth." It was only such heretics as Wyclif who protested against the appalling social order, and his argument was so sound, and the attachment of the people to the Church so feeble, that a writer of the year 1390 says that half the people of England—it would be safe to say a third—followed him in his heresy. But they had dared to attack war and the exploitation of the people, and the Church united with the State to exterminate them.

So it was all over Christian Europe. Eccardus (*Geschichte des niederen Volks*) tells the story of the workers in Germany, Brissot (*Histoire du travail*) in France. The martyrdom of man—of the bulk of the people in every land—continued. With one exception. A struggle with the Popes had ruined the wonderfully prosperous and advanced civilization built up by the Saracens (Arabs) in Sicily, but until the middle of the thirteenth century the Arabs still held most of Spain and Portugal. They had started from the barbaric level several centuries after the Anglo-Saxons, Franks, and Germans, yet by the year 1000 they had in Spain alone more people, and immeasurably happier and more prosperous people, than there were in the whole of Christian Europe. A dozen cities of from quarter of a million to a million people, several of which could have bought up Christendom, with lit and paved streets, sewerage, and admirable sanitary systems, displayed an art, a culture, a complete religious tolerance, and a social idealism that put Europe to shame. Even the tens of thousands of gay white-washed villages rang with song and music, and generally had their schools. But I must tell that wonderful story elsewhere. It must suffice here to indicate that this great Southern civilization, welcoming visitors and scholars from all parts of Europe, was the chief source of inspiration in directing the use of the new wealth and resources of Europe.

CHAPTER VII

SOCIAL VALUE OF THE REFORMATION

IT is part of the new apologetic of the Churches that we must not blame Christianity for the dismal failure of the medieval Church. I have just had the pleasure of a debate with one of their representatives, Dr. A. W. Harrison, Principal of Westminster Training College, whose recent work I analysed in an earlier chapter. In a clear and severely-reasoned half-hour speech I summarized the historical argument which runs through the preceding chapters. I showed that all the supposed inspiration of early Christianity had issued in, to use Lecky's words, " one of the most contemptible periods of history," and that the claim that the new nations of Europe were so refractory to civilization that the Church (or any other agency) could do no more is entirely discredited by three further facts : that the " barbarians " themselves (the Goths, the Lombards, the Franks, the Germans, and the Normans) had made five attempts to restore civilization and had been thwarted by the Church, that Greek Christendom had been as grossly barbarized as Latin, and that sceptical Caliphs had led the equally barbaric Arabs to a high civilization in a century.

These indisputable historical facts were placidly ignored by Dr. Harrison. What Europe then had, he said, was not Christianity. It had lost sight of the teaching of Jesus ; which is in itself a peculiar reflection on the long line of Christian saints and doctors, from Augustine to Aquinas, who shaped the theology of the medieval Church. But when I insisted that the inspirational value of the Gospels must be measured by their success or failure to inspire in the actual historical world, Dr. Harrison, after a few feeble attempts to revive the old legends about abolishing slavery, uplifting woman, etc., began, almost at the last minute—I had ten minutes to reply—to claim that this medieval Church inspired the school-life, the creation of the universities, the splendid art, the literature, etc., of the later Middle Ages. And when I, in the few minutes at my disposal, pointed out that the economic development of Europe and the powerful stimulation of the Arab civilization fully account for these things, as I have shown, he in his final speech, to which I was not permitted to reply, poured out a torrent of claims for Christianity as the inspiration of our real progress during the last century and a half.

In the ninth chapter I shall show that these claims are as fictitious as the claim that early Christianity had tens of thousands of martyrs and broke the fetters of the slave or taught the Romans to have schools and charitable institutions. For the moment the chief point of interest is this : the apologist skipped abruptly from the supposed services of the Church in the thirteenth and fourteenth centuries to its supposed services in the late eighteenth and the nineteenth centuries. He had asked us to believe that Christianity is only really effective when it gets back to the Gospels, yet he could not formulate a single claim of social service for his religion after the Reformation, which is supposed to have been, and in large part was, a return from sacerdotalism to the Gospels !

You will find that a general feature of apologetic works. There are no services to be claimed. My friend, Dr. G. H. Putnam, says in his *Censorship of the Church of Rome*, that the immense literary activity before, during, and after the Reformation made it " an intellectual revolution " : that such vast numbers of even peasants and artisans in Germany devoured the books and pamphlets that you could not to-day find any similarly large body in any country willing to take an interest in thoughtful literature. That is the price one pays for being conciliatory to the Churches and taking the word, as Dr. Putnam did, of clerical advisers. At the very time when he wrote this, several million German workers were keen readers of economic literature, and a few years ago the number had grown to nearly twenty millions.

As to the supposed expansion of education at the time of the Reformation, we can best test it in the case of England. Catholics boast how many schools had been founded before the Reformation. Protestants boast how many thousands they built in the seventeenth and eighteenth centuries. But the fact is, and it was stated in the House of Commons in 1807, that at the beginning of the nineteenth century, after all these centuries of Christian zeal for education, more than ninety per cent of the population, which means virtually the whole of the workers, were illit-

erate.   There were industrial towns of 50,000 people
—Oldham and Ashton, for instance—without a single
school.   And in spite of the coarseness, vice, and
violence which inevitably accompanied this dense
ignorance, the Church opposed every effort to estab-
lish a national system of schools, its chief spokesman,
the Bishop of Exeter, saying in the House of Lords :

> Looking at the poor as a class, they could not expect that
> those who were assigned by Providence to the laborious
> occupations of life should be able largely to cultivate their
> intellects.

We will return later to the fight for education, but
against any claim of either Church to have served the
race in this respect we have to put this brutal fact :
taking Christian Europe as a whole (two or three countries were in advance of England) about the middle of
the eighteenth century, fourteen centuries after the
establishment of Christianity, two centuries after the
Reformation, considerably more than ninety per cent
of the workers could neither read nor write.

Yet that is the most confident claim that is made
for the effect of " the return to the teaching of the
Gospels."   No one is bold enough to claim that the
position of woman improved.   She found, on the contrary, that the system of insulting legal and social
disabilities from which the sceptical nineteenth century freed her was now completed.   No new claim is
made for the inspiration of art.   Indeed, it is one of
the most ironic comments on the claim of a religious
inspiration of medieval art that, when the Reformation and (as Catholics claim) the Counter-Reformation had crushed the sceptical frivolity of the time

and restored religion, art nearly perished. Spain was only just beginning its Renaissance, and the artistic development continued a little longer in that country than in Italy, but by the end of the seventeenth century art and letters were dead in Italy, Spain, and Portugal, and such art as there was in France and England was anything but religious ; while in Germany the religious war blighted all culture for a century. Art perished with its real inspiration : the very fleshy joy of life of people in the fourteenth and fifteenth centuries.

These are inevitable consequences of any sincere return to the Gospels. Art is sensual and seductive : culture leads to pride and heresy. That lesson has been drawn from the Gospels by all the men, from the second century onward, who are recommended to us as the ablest and most devout exponents of Christianity. It is only because our age would not tolerate such a religion that the other-worldly teaching of Jesus is now strained and twisted and made to regard both worlds. The most desperate, and indeed ludicrous, attempts are made to prove that Jesus did not predict the speedy end of the world, and that when he spoke of " everlasting fire," concern about which ought to overwhelm all other concerns, he really meant a temporary condition of moderate discomfort imposed by the sinful soul upon itself. The Reformers, not having such an age as ours to meet, drew the same lesson as the early Fathers. Luther, it is true, being himself a very sensual man, compromised on the subject of personal asceticism ; as Melanchthon and Zwingli compromised on the

D

intellectual side.   But the pure logic of the Reformation appears in Calvin and the Scottish, English, and American Puritans.

Nor can it be claimed even that either the Reformation or the Counter-Reformation effected any permanent improvement of morals.   The latter is, in fact, one of the sorriest myths that our historians have suffered the Jesuits to impose upon them.   Rome was sobered for a time, it is true, but not by virtue.   The first Pope who really tried and desired to reform his Church, Hadrian VI, a Dutchman, was ridiculed into death by the Romans in a year.   Then the cardinals, heavily bribed, put on the throne, to confront Luther, the unscrupulous and worldly Clement VII, a bastard of the Medici family ; and his ambition brought upon Rome such fearful chastisement by the Catholic Spanish and Lutheran German troops that the city is estimated to have lost about £10,000,000 (five times as much as this in modern coinage) in loot and to have had its population reduced by massacre, famine, and plague from 90,000 to 32,000.   It was the most ghastly rape of a city even in those savage times.

It is quite true that now for some time Rome missed the sybaritic opulence which its Popes and cardinals had enjoyed for a century, yet the next two Popes, until 1553, were of the old type.   Paul III was a man who had got the cardinalate because his sister was the mistress of Pope Alexander VI, and he had been for thirty years one of the most immoral of the cardinals.   His successor, Julius III, was a glutton, a heavy gambler, a man suspected of the gravest vices.

But half of Europe was now in revolt, and the sins of Rome had for a time to be pushed out of sight. Then there were several reforming Popes, yet before the end of the sixteenth century the city was as licentious as ever. Rodocanachi shows in his *Courtisanes et buffons* (a study of Roman morals at this time) that the Pope's Vicar, who levied a tax for the Pope on loose women, estimated that by the year 1600 there were again fifteen to sixteen thousand of them—some openly entertaining prelates and rising to £10,000 a year—in Rome ; which means that there were as many of them as there were adult males in " the sacred city." It was the same all over Italy.

In France and Spain the old license grew even worse as the wealth of the countries increased, but we must not suppose that Protestant lands were any better. England passed into the Elizabethan age, then into that of the Stuarts, and need not be discussed. The German world was patchy. In Switzerland the Calvinists substituted their sour vices for those of the Roman Church. In Germany itself and the Scandinavian countries, grossness and license continued. The Jesuit Father Grisar has published a life of Luther and, while much of it is reckless libel, the phrases which he reproduces from *Luther's Table Talk* and *Letters* show that he habitually used speech of the very coarsest description. The Jesuit has to acknowledge that this was the kind of language used in the Augustinian monasteries in which Luther had lived, and the extant sermons of anti-Lutheran preachers like Friar Thomas Murner show that they used these gross words in the pulpit. Luther's word for women, when they sought relief from their disabilities, is vile. Such a man could not, and did not, insist on chastity. In a letter of the year 1525 he says that it is no more in the power of man than working miracles. Though he was not consistent, he often said such things.

This aspect of life I must, as usual, touch briefly and turn to the more important issue of social morals. As few readers will be ignorant of Luther's attitude to the peasants when they rebelled, it is not necessary to say much. The fuel had been prepared by the preaching of the left wing of the Hussites, which resembled that of the more radical Lollards in England, but it was the new practice of reading the Bible during fifty years before the Reformation that kindled the flame. We have now Socialist preachers who find in the Gospels an anticipation of Karl Marx, and even the more aristocratic preacher or apologist represents that they brand all injustice. But the peasants of Germany, which means at least four-fifths of the nation, still lived in the degrading and brutalizing life which I described in the last chapter. Indeed, it was worse in Germany, for serfdom had increased with the substitution of Roman law for old German law. As the news of the new age of evangelical justice spread amongst them there were many revolts, from 1510 onward, and in 1525 the whole country, except Catholic Bavaria, saw armies of thousands of peasants armed with scythes and forks and knives, marching to attack castles and towns.

Their leaders then appealed to Luther to endorse their claim of justice, and he replied with a violent repudiation. In a pamphlet (*Against the Murderous*

Peasants) which he addressed to the princes and nobles he says :

Let all who are able cut them down, slaughter and stab them, openly or in secret, and remember that there is nothing more poisonous, noxious, and utterly devilish than a rebel.

Unquestionably he was playing for the continued friendship of the princes and nobles, who would have willingly returned to the Pope if they felt that evangelicalism meant the disturbance of the workers. But the way in which the horrors of that war are kept out of our literature while the immeasurably less outrages of the French Revolution are thrust upon us every year is a scandal. The " return to the teaching of Jesus " was followed by an orgy of brutality that has no parallel in the history of the Roman Empire. The peasants, from whose brutalized characters one might expect such things—the men whom Dr. Putnam imagines poring devoutly over the Bible a few years before—dealt savagely with the men, women, and often children of the landed aristocracy. But the nobles and their troops retorted with equal savagery. Molten pitch and sulphur were poured upon the peasants, and those who were taken alive were barbarously tortured and mutilated. One batch of eighty-two peasants had their eyes cut out. Of an army of 8,000, who were retreating, 5,000 were killed. Their bodies hung from trees all over Germany. In the district of Zabern in Alsace, 16,242 peasants were so hastily buried that the stench kept travellers away for years. In that one summer 150,000 persons, mostly peasants, were killed, often with revolting savagery ; and the writers who warn the world against irreligion by exaggerating the massacre of 2,000 priests and aristocrats during three years of the French Revolution, never mention this orgy of evangelical brutality. The flesh of some rebel leaders was torn off with red-hot pincers.

Luther had written that even the peasants' demand for the abolition of serfdom was " against the Gospels and robbery." The more cultivated Melanchthon, to whom also they appealed, urged the nobles to " keep them down more severely than ever." And this interpretation of the gospel-message was drastically carried out. " The arm of the prince and the noble everywhere became longer, swifter, and firmer," says the German social historian Eccardus. But the whole of central Europe was soon involved in the religious Thirty Years' War (1618–48), in which there was a similar return to barbarism from Bohemia to the Baltic.

After the taking of Magdeburg by Tilly, the profoundly religious leader of the Catholic troops, the men were let loose upon the citizens. " The soldier must have some reward," said Tilly when a few horrified officers protested. In the ruins of one church were found the bodies of 53 women raped and beheaded. All the girls and women were raped, babies were flung upon the burning buildings or stabbed, and every house was looted. Of 30,000 citizens, men, women, and children, only about 4,000 were spared. Gustavus Adolphus alone refused this reward of a victory to his soldiers. The land was stripped bare when a Catholic army of 34,000 soldiers, with 127,000 prostitutes (who were largely women beggared by the war) and camp-followers, moved across it like a swarm of locusts. That was one of many armies, and there were times when their advanced guard surprised some group of the wild and fugitive peasants sitting round a cauldron in which they cooked the flesh of some soldier they had trapped or even of a criminal stolen from the gibbet. Such were the savage massacres and the inroads of plague and famine that the population of Bohemia was reduced from 4,000,000 to 900,000. All central Europe was exhausted and demoralized for a century, until the enlightened reign of the sceptical Frederic the Great began.

Such facts make a mockery of the modern distinction between what the Churches did and what the teaching of the Gospels would do. Before there was any Church, in the modern sense, the early Christians passed into the fierce struggle of Gnostics and anti-Gnostics, and by the beginning of the third century we find them completely demoralized in the Roman and African communities. Then, when medieval sacerdotalism is destroyed over half of Europe, and the Bible is distributed and read everywhere, we get these unspeakable horrors of the religious war ; for, whatever political interests we may now detect in it, the main issue was the triumph of Catholicism or Protestantism. Clearly the Gospel ethic is set in a frame of doctrine which ruins the promise of its better qualities. One of the most frequent unconscious ironies of the modern apologist is when he reproduces the words which someone is supposed to have said in early times, " See how these Christians love one another," and boasts that his religion alone inspires an effective doctrine of brotherhood. How vastly different is the record from that of Buddhism.

And if it be said that the war-passions (themselves aroused by religion) choked the Christian belief of half of Europe at this time, consider what social effect the Reformation had in other countries. Thorold Rogers, the best authority, shows that the condition of the worker was worse after the Reformation in England. A wealth of which men in Europe had never dreamed—though it was still far below that of Arab lands and was paltry in comparison with ours— began to flush the veins of the nation, but the worker did not share it. As prices rose there was, Thorold Rogers says, " a conspiracy of the lawyers " to prevent the workers from combining to secure an increase of wages. The anti-combination laws, with their savage sentences, were passed to protect wealth, and the workers experienced a new type of slavery. The population increased more rapidly, and labour became more abundant and cheaper. The Civil War, reducing the supply of labour, led to a temporary improvement, but after 1740 the workers passed again into the deplorable state in which we shall find them in the ninth chapter.

It was the same in every country. The Catholic who would find an argument in this deterioration in England after the Reformation may be recommended to read Brissot's exact study of what happened to the French workers. They still had their guilds in the sixteenth century, and these helped to complete their ruin. In a word, Brissot shows, the wage of the

French agricultural worker fell from one franc and a half in the fifteenth century to half a franc at the time of the Revolution ; and prices rose, and the nobles cut down the ancient rights of the peasant to take timber, game, etc. The wage of the artisan sank from three francs fifteen centimes to two francs twenty centimes, and the purchasing power of money sank by one half. In Catholic Spain and Portugal the thirty million happy and prosperous folk of Moorish days shrank to six million impoverished and densely ignorant people, exploited by Church and State. In Italy the retro-gression was almost as bad. And Popes, bishops, and theologians were as dumb, and as comfortable and generally frivolous, as the English bishops.

Indeed, all the nations, Catholic and Protestant, now joined in a viler social injustice than could be found anywhere in the pagan world at the time when Christianity came to power. I have already pointed out that the common idea that slavery was extin-guished in Europe during the Middle Ages and restored in Protestant days is wholly wrong. Slavery shrank, from the causes which I gave, but it was never con-demned. A large slave-trade was still conducted by those Christian nations which found it profitable when, in the second half of the fifteenth century, the advance of the Turks destroyed their commerce. But simul-taneously the Spaniards and Portuguese, who now expelled the last of the Moors and took their com-manding place in navigation, began to kidnap ship-loads of Africans. The discovery of America soon afterwards led to the last and vilest expansion of the ancient evil.

It would have been amazing if no one in Christendom at this late date felt qualms about this brutality, but the Spanish theologians whom Isabella consulted could reply only that the Church had never condemned slavery. In point of fact, the Spanish and Portuguese had already virtually enslaved the American natives and were threatening to exterminate them by their ruthless exploitations, and the missionaries, seeing their " converts " disappear, pressed for the use of black labour. The English and French joined in the profitable trade as eagerly as the Spaniards and Portuguese. In conditions of such callous brutality that often half the Africans died on the voyage, about ten million blacks were conveyed to America during the seventeenth and eighteenth centuries. I need not tell again the horrible story. It is enough that, as one of the leading apologists, the Rev. Loring Brace, says (*Gesta Christi*, p. 365), " the guilt of this great crime rests on the Christian Church as an organized body." What there is in their claim to have helped in abolishing it we shall see later.

It is difficult to see what claim can be made of social service of the new form of Christianity, with all its insistence on the reading of the Gospels. Every authority on the condition of the workers proves that it deteriorated. Every competent feminist historian shows that woman's legal and social position was not improved. The historian of education speaks of the opening of many schools, but he admits that the workers remained almost universally illiterate. The historian of morals describes England (apart from the Puritan episode), Germany, Denmark, and Scandinavia, enjoying just the same license as in the fifteenth century; and, if any be disposed to stress the personal virtue of Puritan periods, he should read Buckle on the prevalence of vice among the Scots and Rupert Brooke on the same prevalence in New England. In England, it is true, the Puritan party at first (when many sceptics belonged to it) promised to make a needed contribution to the building of English character. One of the best of them, James Harrington, wrote a social utopian work, *Oceana*, on the model of Plato and More. But it displeased Cromwell and found no favour amongst the strict Puritans. A fanatical zeal for personal morals absorbed all their energy and gave rise to a general sourness, narrowness, and so much hypocrisy that the nation recovered its freedom with ease when Cromwell died.

This was the common experience. The fervent evangelical who objects that the Church of England was no more representative of Christianity than the Church of Rome will look in vain for the appearance of any zeal for social justice amongst the strict Calvinists of Geneva. What he will find instead is such fanaticism for the doctrinal frame in which the Christian ethic is set that that particular enthusiast for the words of Jesus, Calvin, interpreted his doctrine of brotherhood to mean that heretics must be burned at the stake in the brutal medieval manner. Amongst the Calvinists of Scotland it would be ludicrous to look for social service. The condition of the workers was fouler even than in England, large bodies of them, such as the coal and salt-workers, living in a state of veritable slavery. The great body had so depressing and brutalizing a life that, in spite of the ferocious sermons on hell, one of the leading Protestant historians says (Chambers, *Domestic Annals of Scotland*, II, 42) that sodomy itself was so rife that it " makes the daylight profligacy of the subsequent reign shine white in comparison." The subsequent reign was the extraordinarily licentious period of Charles II.

CHAPTER VIII

RELIGION AND THE FRENCH REVOLUTION

A NEW era in the history of the race opened in the second half of the eighteenth century, and the French Revolution may justly be taken as its first definite expression. It is a painful comment on the way in which we still write and teach history that the vast majority of us, cultivated or merely literate, think of this Revolution as a morbid and horrible eruption of mob-brutality. The truth is that a large and detailed work on the genuine social history of Christendom is badly needed. I do but sketch here the lines which such a work would inevitably follow. A complete study would be even more drastic, and would show that the statements which our religious literary men are permitted to impose upon the public, the conventional estimates of religious influence which adorn our editorials, are as false as the stories of the early saints and martyrs.

It is an amiable and graceful pastime to turn over the pages of this past history and pick out here and there a picture of some upright abbot or bishop who, for a few decades, saw that justice was done in his little area, some saint who really acted as if all men were his brothers. But it is a poor sort of education when there are a thousand narrowly fanatical or unjust or dissipated abbots or bishops for every one whom we can admire. It reminds us of writers who ask us to admire a Church which (from religious motives) induces the bandits of the Middle Ages to suspend their brutalities for a week at Christmas (the Truce of God) but never condemns war, and uses or inspires it thousands of times in its own interest. The social service to the race of any agency or organization must be decided by a balance of good and evil. You do not count the copper which a thief drops into a blind man's box if he takes out a sixpence or a shilling. I could quote from genuine history a hundred instances of brutality, injustice, disservice to the race on a broad scale for every edifying page that is reproduced, very often from the lives of saints or other fraudulent documents, from the history of Christendom. Here I have confined myself to significant or typical illustrations and broad influences.

In approaching a period of real progress we should remind ourselves that the life-experience itself has in every age and clime brought about such an advance. We find it in India in the age of Asoka, who applied the humanitarian principles evolved in the ferment of the seventh century B.C. and several times in the periods of revival in China. But it is a familiar phenomenon in the story of every civilization and is wholly independent of the prevailing religious system. We should therefore expect that Europe, even if it cut itself off from the lessons of earlier civilizations, would evolve a higher ideal from its own rich experience from the twelfth to the eighteenth century. Most of us smile when we are asked to entertain the childish theory that the rapid progress of our age is due to our better understanding of the teaching of Christ. That is a theme for Sunday Schools and Bible Classes. The ultimate root of our advance since the middle of the eighteenth century is experience of life, or the new spirit of directly consulting life instead of ancient prophets and documents ; and the extraordinary failure of Europe to profit by seven centuries of tense experience before that date is one more proof of the disservice of Christianity.

For European life was still more than streaked with barbarism at the middle of the eighteenth century. The highest authority on English life at that time, the *Cambridge Medieval History* (Vol. VI), says:

> The masses were ignorant and brutalized. . . . The government pandered to mob passions by public executions and by unworthy concessions to mob violence and insulted humanity by the brutal ferocity of the criminal code.

Is it not time that we dropped the word " mob " when we are referring to four-fifths or more of the nation ? And it was not the " mob " that made the criminal code or was responsible for the savagery of " the bloods," the disgusting state of the marriage law, the duelling and gambling, the corruption of court and parliament, and a hundred other evils. Dean Inge, who dislikes our materialistic age, professes to admire that of Queen Anne, the life of which continued under the Georges. Thackeray knew that age and he said :

> You could no more suffer in a British drawing-room under the reign of Queen Victoria a fine gentleman or a fine lady of Queen Anne's time, or hear what they heard and said, than you would receive an ancient Briton.

You certainly could not say that of the Roman patricians of the fourth century. But we shall find life barbarous enough at the beginning of the nineteenth century. Let us turn to France.

The appalling selfishness, callousness to the sufferings of the people, and unbridled extravagance and profligacy of the French court, aristocracy, and prelates from Louis XIV to the Revolution are well known, but I would advise the reading of a recent work by a Catholic member of the French Academy, Louis Bertrand's *Private Life of Louis XIV*. I will quote only that Bertrand asks us to be lenient on the ground that the king was for between ten and fifteen years drenched with aphrodisiacs by the agents of his mistress and suffered from satyriasis. Certainly the most lurid pages of Roman history during the short reigns of a few emperors do not rival the pages of aristocratic French history for a hundred years ; and the Roman crowd did not include bishops and cardinals.

But, if you read French, turn to the Appendix to the thirteenth volume of Martin's *History of France* for the reverse of the picture. He gives the documents relating to a great famine from 1650 to 1656, just before Louis began to build the Versailles Palace. Hundreds of thousands died of starvation, when they had eaten up their dogs, cats, rats, and any growing thing that looked edible. They dug up dead dogs and horses, ate their clothes, and even bit into their own flesh. In one small city there were 600 entirely naked orphans. Yet the king's officials pursued them everywhere for taxes and drove them out to die by the thousand in the woods. From such soil sprang the glorious Palace of Versailles ; and the bishops buried " the great Monarch," the " Sun King," and his successors with superb flattery.

No one who knows what the workers of France suffered during two centuries and how brutalized they must have been wonders that there were outrages ; though, as we shall see, the number of those who perpetrated or approved outrages has been grossly exaggerated. The revolutionary advance came, as advances always come, from experience of life. We to-day proudly accept the charge that the " philosophers " were responsible for the revolution : not so much the Deists of the earlier generation, Voltaire and Rousseau, as the men who, like Diderot, D'Alembert, and Holbach, all atheists, translated their humanitarian ideals—for Voltaire's profound humanity (finely shown by Mr. Arliss in his film) had nothing to do with his academic belief in God—into practicable proposals and protests. How all this ultimately came from Deism, and that from the classical revival, cannot be discussed here. It is enough that a body of deistic and atheistic nobles and commoners (Mirabeau, Lafayette, Desmoulins, Talleyrand, Sieyes, etc.), with a few radical priests and Catholics, resisted the king's last attempt at despotism in the summer of 1789 and carried an almost bloodless revolution. That the intoxicated people broke into a few outrages in Paris and many in the provinces is not surprising. The middle-class and noble representatives of the people would never have succeeded without the support of an armed nation.

The popular idea of the French Revolution is maintained by (against all historical usage) making that name cover a period of five years. The Revolution itself occurred in the summer of 1789, and it was milder than the American Revolution which inspired it. The French accepted a constitutional monarchy and left the Church established and endowed. The leading prelates and nobles accepted it (August 4) and solemnly surrendered all their privileges. And the evils that followed are mainly due to two causes. First, the bishops and nobles repented their surrender and fled abroad to implore the Pope to brand the Declaration of the Rights of Man " insane " and beg the monarchs of Austria, Prussia, and England to destroy the French government and secure the return of their privileges. The second is that the admirable statesmen who wrought the Revolution and guided the new State bloodlessly for three years took a self-denying oath in 1791 to retire from office, and they thus innocently let in men of no experience and often of poor character.

But what followed is totally misrepresented by novelists, essayists, and even historians who are not experts on the period. French historians of great ability have in the last sixty years sorted out their legends and documents, and I must be content to give here, very briefly, the more important of their findings, as stated in Lavisse's authoritative history and the works of Professor A. Aulard. As to outrages, which began with the September Massacres of 1792, more than three years after the Revolution—there was no guillotine in France until 1792—it is agreed that about 20,000 were killed in two and a half years, though only about 17,000 cases are definitely known. That is less than the Catholics of Paris had butchered, for no offence but religion, in a few days in the St. Bartholomew Massacre, of which no one now speaks. It is *twenty times less* than the number of unarmed men, women, and children put to death by Catholic monarchs and " mobs," with the approval and in most cases direct encouragement of the Catholic hierarchy, between 1798 and 1870 ; of which also no one speaks. I will show that in the next chapter. It is not certainly a larger number than that of the revolutionaries killed, generally with great barbarity, by the Catholics in a few months after the fall of Robespierre and, later, the fall of Napoleon ; and of that, again, no one ever speaks.

Further, it is now fully established that the excuse of the revolutionaries—that there was a dangerous royalist plot in the country—is at all events a statement of fact. In a recent study, Jean Barruol has shown· that at the fall of Robespierre " sixty-four Departments, prepared by the counter-revolutionaries, rose in revolt." A force of 20,000 royalists appeared at once at Lyons alone, and over the whole of the southern provinces there was a reign of terror. Martin says that " many thousands " were killed, and that " the counter-revolution had a mixture of cold cruelty and depravity which was more hideous than the brutal ferocity of the Jacobin Terrorists." But of all this, again, no one ever speaks.

Finally, the popular idea that the victims of the revolutionaries were mainly priests, nuns, and aristocrats is grotesque. Of the victims of the September massacres, who numbered 1,110 (instead of the 15,000 of clerical rumour), not more than 450 were priests and aristocrats according to Walter's recent study (*Les massacres de Septembre*, 1932). Lavisse says 366. The majority of the victims were criminals and prostitutes. It was neither the government nor the people of Paris who wrought these outrages, but a few hundred butchers and other ignorant workers, mainly Catholics, who wanted to " purify Paris " as well as get rid of spies. The Cambridge History estimates that during the whole fifteen months of terror 2,628 were guillotined at Paris, and it adds that it would be " ludicrous " to believe that the killers represented more than a few thousand out of the half-million folk of Paris. You will hardly find a man or woman who does not know how the women of the people at Paris —women kept illiterate and stunted by Church and State—knitted socks while the courts pronounced sentence of death ; but not one of us was ever told by our novelists and film-producers, our Chestertons and Bellocs, how, in the reaction, the educated ladies of Naples and Madrid did their silk-embroidery in court while even more savage sentences were passed.

Few will not be surprised to hear that it is now established that the great majority of the victims of the Revolution, or of the years 1792–4, were working men, who fell in the violent quarrels of parties. The analysis of the 17,000 definitely known cases shows that sixty-seven per cent were working men, twelve per cent were middle-class men, eight per cent were priests and nuns, and six per cent were aristocrats (largely members of the secret royalist conspiracy). Deplorable as these executions were, they are mild in comparison with the appalling massacres perpetrated a few years later by the royalist-clericals, as I will show. Nor does any writer on these matters care to tell his readers how these priests and aristocrats had lit up a savage civil war in the western provinces which drew off large armies and cost the lives of 200,000 Frenchmen just at the time when every man was needed to repel the invaders in the east.

I give these facts, which are now fully established and accepted, because it is to-day a very popular trick of Christian apologetics to claim that the horrors of the French Revolution are a practical illustration of what any people will do without the restraining influence of Christianity and are therefore essential in a consideration of its social service. So recklessly is this apologetic work done, and so readily are its claims repeated in our journals and popular literature, that there is actually more talk to-day about the horrors of the Revolution, just when historians have exposed the grossness of the calumnies, than there was fifty years ago. But I must conclude this matter briefly, since this is only one page in the deeply significant and little-known story of the last hundred and fifty years.

The apologetic legend, which you will find repeated at some time or other in the editorials of every paper in England, is that the revolutionary leaders " deprived the people of their religion " and massacres and awful blasphemies followed. The prostitute-on-an-altar story is an even worse piece of fiction than the others. Contemporary Parisian papers and witnesses unanimously report that the Feast of Reason and Liberty which was celebrated in the cathedral of Notre Dame in 1793 was a ceremony of great dignity and decorum. The clergy of the cathedral had resigned their functions and handed over the edifice. The altars were draped and not used. The lady who impersonated Liberty (not a goddess of Reason) is not known with certainty, but is one of three known ladies and very probably a leading actress from the Operá (which organized the pageant). And what she did was, not to sing a ribald song, but to recite with great dignity the poet Chenier's fine ode to Liberty. Yet the old legend, which is a lie in every syllable, is repeated even in historical works of the last few years.

And this is not the whole of the mendacity. Decorous as the pageant was, and although the bishop and clergy of the cathedral had renounced their office, the government refused to countenance it. Roman Catholicism was still the established religion of France, and Danton and Robespierre, instead of depriving the people of their religion, were furiously assailed by the people week after week with public demands for the disestablishment of the Church, yet they refused. Even when the churches were closed by the priests and people themselves, or converted into Temples of Liberty, in nearly all parts of France, the atheist Danton refused to consent. As for Robespierre, he protested that atheism was the creed of the aristocrats and, when he removed Danton, he made his own deistic Cult of the Supreme Being the national religion. Thus the French people were, against their will, forced

by their leaders to have a national religion all through
the terror, and it was under the ensign of Unitarianism
that the last few bloody months were passed. The
Catholics, as I said, massacred many thousands when
Robespierre fell, but a new government or Directorate
put an end to all the sanguinary quarrels and gave
the country peace ; *and this was the only period between the Revolution and Napoleon when France had no
religion.*

Most of my readers will agree with me, since these
facts are now entirely accepted in serious history, that
a reconstruction of the story of Christendom, ancient
and modern, is urgently needed. But let us get back
to the direct line of our inquiry and see the Revolution
as merely the most dramatic expression, ruined by the
excesses of political fanatics, of a great forward movement of the race. From the middle of the eighteenth
century, as I said, the world was preparing to advance.
The American Revolution may be conceived as a
political resentment of tyranny, but the movement of
ideas which found expression in the Constitution—the
ideas of sceptics and deists like Franklin, Paine, Jefferson, and Adams—was an organic part of a world-
movement. Voltaire had learned his liberal ideas, as
Paine did, in London, and the new spirit went so far
that during the war with America liberal leaders like
Fox defiantly wore the colours of the rebels in the
House, and the citizens of London and Bristol refused
the king's request to raise regiments. France, we
saw, made simultaneous and even greater progress.
Germany witnessed the revolt against tradition that
produced Goethe and Schiller. Spain under Count d'

Aranda, Portugal under the Marquis de Pombal, and Naples under the liberal Tannucci made almost equal progress and seethed with ideas and plans of reform. In 1773 these liberal statesmen induced their Catholic monarchs to force the Pope to condemn and suppress the Jesuits : an event which in the religious world was felt much as the fall of the Bastille would be later in the political world.

Let us be quite clear that this was a movement of social reform. It aimed at securing constitutional monarchy—republicanism was entertained by very few even in America until the revolt was well on its way—and ending the feudal tyranny of kings and nobles. It demanded the representation of the people and a share in making the laws. It called for a purification (as voiced by Beccaria and his followers) of law and penal procedure from its grossness. It gave birth to the demand for the emancipation of woman, as set out by Mary Wollstonecraft, Mme. Condorcet, and others. It attacked slavery. It demanded the education of the people as the proper means to end the coarseness in which they had lived for ages. It took up the attack upon war which Erasmus and Grotius had begun. It was, in short, from beginning to end a moderate demand of liberty and justice, of enlightenment, free discussion, and complete freedom of conscience. These are the springs of our modern civilization.

This first real forward movement in Christendom was checked everywhere by the excesses of the French revolutionaries, which, grossly exaggerated and distorted—the number of victims was put as high as

700,000—gave a pretext for the appalling reaction, which lasted until about 1830. What was the relation of Christianity to the forward movement and to the repression of it ? Here it is not necessary to enlarge much. It is only the popular apologists who make such claims as that all our modern reforms sprang from a more devout study of the Gospels. Nine-tenths at least of the leaders of this movement were either Deists, who thrust the Bible entirely aside, or Atheists ; and they were bitterly opposed both by Protestant and Catholic Churches everywhere.

In dealing with personalities of that age it is often very difficult to distinguish between Deists and Atheists. A Mirabeau or a Napoleon, even a dog-matic materialist like Jefferson, would use the word God and not mean much more than an Atheist like Shelley or a Pantheist like Goethe. Since both philo-sophies were anti-Christian, we need not here try to distinguish. In France the majority of the leaders were Atheists, with a few Deists like Lafayette and Robespierre and a very few Catholics. Pombal, D'Aranda, and Tannucci were at the most Deists and were hated by the clergy, who wrecked their work. Franklin, Paine, Washington, Adams, Jefferson, and Hamilton were Deists. Pitt (until the reaction) and Fox were Deists—and both probably nearer atheism —and of ten Englishmen who, in their various ways, led the reform-movement in this country—Wilkes, Priestley, Horne Tooke, Godwin, Mary Wollstonecraft, Paine, Shelley, Holcroft, and Hardy—eight were Deists or Atheists and one a Unitarian.

But since the only serious claim for the Church in

the advance of the eighteenth century is that in the person of William Wilberforce it led the movement for the abolition of slavery, I will conclude with a few words on this.   No one wishes to deny that a few prominent Churchmen and Quakers joined in the movement.   It would be an amazing confession of the futility of the Christian conscience if none even of the educated laity of the Church recognized the evil of the crime when radicals and Quakers began to denounce it.   But the almost universal claim that Wilberforce's Christian conscience led him to see the evil and start a movement for abolition is as false as all the other claims.

Here I need not profess to have made any discovery or put a new and disputable interpretation upon the facts.   They are frankly stated, largely in his own words, by his sons, both clergymen of the Church of England, in their biography of him.   An uncle had tried to make a Methodist of him in his boyhood, and his mother (who seems to have been remarkably liberal) brought him away and deliberately substituted the love of pleasure in his mind for religion.   He speaks himself in his diary (quoted in the biography, I, p. 6) of "the dreadful effects of the efforts afterwards [after his twelfth year] used but too successfully to wean me from all religion."   In that mood he remained until he was nearly thirty, and his sons admit that he for a long time refused to take a degree at Cambridge (where his friends were all of the liberal group) because he could not conscientiously sign the Thirty-Nine Articles.   Yet, they tell us, it was in this stage and set that he learned to attack slavery.   At the age of fourteen (1773) he wrote a fiery paper against it for a York paper. In a letter of the year 1783 he says that his " moral and religious principles are such as in these days are not very generally prevalent " (p. 32). He was a Deist, and his warmest friend was the younger Pitt, who, like his father Lord Chatham, Sir R. Walpole, and Fox, was at the most a weak sort of Deist.

This is not all. Wilberforce became a Christian, and his great work for abolition falls in his Christian days though he had reached his ideal in his sceptical and frivolous days. But the abolition of slavery across the ocean—English judges had long before declared it illegal in England—was his only social service, and against it we must put a lamentable amount of disservice. He supported Pitt in every phase of his reactionary measures against liberalism, defended him in his vile treatment of radicals and his opposition to the reform of Parliament, and was one of the worst enemies of the workers when they fought for trade unions and the betterment of their condition. He was very liberal with alms, but he unctuously repeated the Christian tag about " the condition in which the Almighty had placed them." One has to smile when one reads a modern Protestant apologist boasting to the workers of what the Church did for them through Wilberforce and Shaftesbury. They happen to be the two men who confess in their Diaries that they had to barricade their houses against the workers of London, who hated them.

Slavery was first abolished by those " wicked and bloodthirsty Atheists of the French Revolution." That was in 1791, forty-two years before England.

Of the abolition-movement in America one need not speak to-day. The Church in the south was solid in justification of slavery, pointing out that Scripture nowhere condemned it, and Mr. Brace admits that even the Churches of the north were " arrayed against true Christianity." The non-Christian abolitionists like Lloyd Garrison (an Agnostic) and Lincoln (a Deist) and their Quaker friends were so hampered that, as Theodore Parker said, " if the whole American Church had dropped through the continent and disappeared altogether, the anti-slavery cause would have been further on." The Baptists owned 225,000 slaves, the Methodists 250,000. Mr. Brace says that even the British Society for the Propagation of the Gospel owned slaves in the West Indies. And Canon Streeter thinks that its share in the abolition of black slavery is the one social service that redeems the Christian record in modern times!

CHAPTER IX

THE STRUGGLE IN THE NINETEENTH CENTURY

On an earlier page I quoted Canon Streeter, one of the ablest of living apologists, saying that, with the exception of the abolition of black slavery (about which he is very gravely wrong), it is " the greatest blot on the history of the Church in modern times" that the leaders of reform were rarely Christian and the Christian leaders almost always opposed them. We have now to see that he is correct in his statement of fact, and, if this is so, the Christian apologetic is reduced to almost the last stage of beggary. For no sophistry can here obscure the issue. If it be true that the idealism which began in the eighteenth century and bore fruit in the nineteenth, the idealism which has raised Europe back to the level of civilization, came predominantly from Deists and Atheists who ignored the New Testament, the Christian claim fails. But if it is further true that the various branches of the Christian Church opposed these reformers, caused an appalling massacre of those who worked for the reforms, and retarded the triumph of those reforms for fifty or a hundred years—a different period in different countries—we have a final proof of my contention that

Christianity actually hindered the recivilization of Europe.

Let me illustrate why such conclusions bear for many people an air of novelty or eccentricity. It has for years been my hope to find leisure to write a history of the struggle in the last century of the various peoples of Europe for freedom of discussion and self-government. No such history exists, and many of the most poignant national chapters of the story are barely or not at all mentioned in our manuals. Our people, for instance, are easily persuaded to regard the South Italian as a surviving medieval type—" the *dolce far niente*, you know," we say with a smile—and the Spaniard as a gay but gracefully indolent character whose favourite word is *mañana*. Do you know that in the last decade of the eighteenth century there was, in proportion to population, more liberal idealism in the kingdom of Naples (south Italy and Sicily) than in England ? Have you ever read that according to the best contemporary Neapolitan historians 250,000 of these liberals of Naples, mostly unarmed, of both sexes and all conditions, were barbarously killed in the struggle for their ideals, and that that is why Naples became what it is ? Recent events have enabled us to correct the ideas of many in regard to Spain. But how many yet know that Spain made the longest and not the least heroic struggle for these reforms of all the peoples of Europe and sacrificed at least 50,000 lives, mostly of unarmed men and women ?

In short, I wrote my history some months ago— publishers decline it with thanks, some saying that it is not good taste to recall these facts to-day—and found, rather to my own astonishment, that between 1795 and 1870 (though the carnage does not stop there) France, Italy, Austria, Spain, and Portugal alone saw at least 300,000 of their finest-spirited men and women executed, murdered, or done to death in foul jails and penal colonies in the cause of humanity, or immeasurably more than were martyred for any other cause whatever in any century of history ; and, needless to say, I am not counting armed republican revolts against a monarch. And here, for my present purpose, is the main point : except in the early years of the Neapolitan struggle, when numbers of bishops and priests joined the people, the Church everywhere not only supported but egged on the monarchs and soldiers to commit every barbarity, often in spite of the most solemn oaths, in order to annihilate liberalism, which was simply a demand for political justice (constitutional monarchy), legal justice (reform of barbaric laws and punishments), social justice (freedom of conscience and discussion), the education of the people, and some improvement of the condition of the workers.

The history of Europe from 1794, when the reaction to the French Revolution may be said to begin, to 1870 (and much later in Russia, Spain, and Portugal), which it is such bad taste to recall, is one of the most really instructive sections of the social record of Christianity. Limitations of space here compel me almost to confine myself to events in England, but a few paragraphs must be devoted to other countries. And, since the truculent reaction began first in Naples and was there particularly repulsive, let me briefly summarize the facts, as told by General Colletta, who was at the time an officer in the Neapolitan army, and the continuer of his history. For the last phase Gladstone endorses the indictment from his own observation.

In 1793 the Queen's spies reported that practically the whole educated class were " Jacobins," and the king, a brutal and dissipated man, executed many and sent thousands to jail. The French interrupted this by taking Naples, but at their departure orders were given to exterminate liberals. Brigands who drank their blood from skulls were enlisted in the work. Human vermin were permitted to roast and eat, under the palace windows, the bodies of liberals they had slain. Thirty thousand were packed into the foul jails; but they were comparatively fortunate, for 40,000 wild troops and bandits were let loose for some days upon the homes, wives, and children of the others. Twenty nobles and three bishops were amongst the hundreds who were hanged.

Napoleon's campaign in Italy put a stop to the carnage, and after Waterloo the Powers permitted the butcher to return to his throne only on condition that he would rule constitutionally. At the altar, surrounded by his bishops, the king took the oath, and he in addition called upon God to strike him dead if he did not mean it " this time," as he said. It was his second oath. And his Church and the Pope sonorously went on with their blessings when he, within a few months, got an Austrian army to crush his humanitarians, and thousands again were slaughtered.

By 1825, says Colletta, " one hundred thousand Nea-politans have perished by every kind of death in the cause of political freedom " ; and the Neapolitan his-torian who then takes up the record claims that 150,000 were killed in the next thirty years. We may assume that the figure is at least half as high. But I cannot go into the barbarous details. As late as 1850 Mr. Gladstone visited Naples and made England shudder at the horrors. Ironically, in a famous phrase, he called the royal-clerical government of Naples " the negation of God." People had thought that this applied only to the French Revolution.

In the Papal States or Papal Kingdom I estimate that from ten to twenty thousand martyrs—or twenty times as many as all the Christian martyrs of the first three centuries—were made by the Popes in thirty years. There were massacres of unarmed men and women by troops led by cardinals ; there were fever-sodden dungeons in which men condemned for twenty years were chained to the wall, and the chain was never undone for any purpose : there were ghastly fortresses in which noble ladies were herded with the male prisoners under male jailors ; there were hun-dreds of executions, and torture was habitually used to extract denunciations of others. And these men had merely wanted a reform of what even Catholic historians (see the Cambridge History) admit to have been the most corrupt and incompetent government in Europe. Less than eighty years ago the Popes were showing all the world that this was, in practice, their idea of social and political ethics. Now they are widely respected as world-oracles, wise with the

E

wisdom of ages . . . Even Mr. Wells prefers the
Papal Church to any other in his autobiography and
is quite tender about it.

The rest must be told in chapter-headings.   In
Portugal another Catholic (and very depraved) monarch
swore a solemn oath in the presence of his God and his
bishops to respect the Constitution if they let him
resume his throne ; and in five years, with just such
barbarity as had been shown in Naples, 17,000 were
executed or murdered and 50,000 sent to the deadly
jails and penal colonies, which for large numbers was
sentence of death.

In Spain, where the people had set up a moderate
Constitution before Napoleon fell, King Ferdinand
(who had a curious resemblance to Nero in his vices,
follies, and cruelties) was admitted back to his throne
after swearing to respect the Constitution.   Within
two years thousands were executed or murdered and
tens of thousands packed in the noisome jails.   In
short, though there was no *armed* revolt in Spain until
1868, about 150,000 Spaniards had suffered for their
humanitarian faith to that time, and at least a third of
these were executed or murdered or died in foul jails
on penal colonies.   The clergy themselves organized
a Society of the Exterminating Angel and let its murderous members loose upon unarmed liberals all over
Spain.   The extermination was carried out with
veritable savagery—read Major Hume's history of
Spain if you doubt me—and the vilest medieval tortures were used in the jails ; and, as I showed in my
Martyrdom of Ferrer, were still being used in Spanish
jails at the beginning of this century.

In France, apart from the thousands who were butchered by Catholic mobs after the fall of Robespierre and the fall of Napoleon, most of the deaths occurred in the revolutionary fighting of 1830 and 1848, when more than 15,000 were shot. But France also had its thousands of quite innocent victims. The promise of Louis XVIII to take no reprisals was worth no more than the oaths of Ferdinand of Spain and Miguel of Portugal. The oath of Louis Philippe, sworn in all the solemnity of Notre Dame, to observe the Constitution was trampled under foot in a few months and thousands suffered ; and the other perjured Louis, Napoleon III, sent 100,000 to death, jail, penal colonies, and exile. In each case the clergy lined up behind the butcher and blessed all his work.

Austria, which until the middle of the last century included the north of Italy as well as Hungary, added tens of thousands to the humanitarian martyrs, not counting the tens of thousands who died fighting. It also used torture habitually. Poland—to turn in conclusion to the Greek variety of Catholicism—added further tens of thousands, though for the first twenty years of the struggle they asked only the rights granted in their Constitution. As to Russia, no man can count the victims from 1820 to 1910, but 100,000 would be a moderate estimate. As late as 1910 there were 174,000 men, women, youths, and girls packed into the jails, one to two hundred committing suicide every month, and hundreds dying of typhus and dysentery.

Leave out Russia and Poland, if you like, and you

have the social record of the Holy Roman Church, which we are asked to respect, not in the days of the Inquisition, but in the days of our grandfathers. What occurred in Protestant lands does not remotely approach the Catholic record in savagery, treachery, and massacre. In England and Germany, it is true, the authorities could not, if they would, have done such things, but let us have some regard for facts in our affections. Making my estimates in each country on the same careful scale, I find that between 1799 and 1870 alone the Catholic monarchs, with the full approval of their bishops, took the lives (by execution, licensed mob-murder, or lethal imprisonment) of at least 300,000 unarmed men, women, youths, and girls, and there were probably nothing like 10,000 such martyrs in all the Protestant lands of Europe put together.

Yet the record of the Protestant Churches is infamous enough, and we will consider it in the case of this country. First, we will summarize what is called the political struggle. Let us understand its nature. By all the leaders in the struggle the " vote " (which was at that time a venal matter, a popular joke) was regarded only as a means to an end. They wanted power to reform the extraordinarily corrupt political and electoral system, to secure a national scheme of education, to reform the law and the sordid penal practice, to destroy all instruments of tyranny, to abolish slavery in the colonies, and to lift the disabilities of the workers. It was a comprehensive humanitarian ideal, and several of the leaders wanted also the substitution of arbitration for war, the emancipation of woman, the reform of the marriage-law, the abolition of the press-tax, and many other reforms.

I have already given the names of the leaders in the eighteenth century and noted that the majority were Atheists and that Wilberforce was one of their most stubborn opponents. One of the funniest cries of modern reactionaries is that a new spirit of revolt has been born of modern scepticism, and they sigh for the placid days of faith. That is the sort of thing we hear as long as it is considered bad taste to tell the truth about even recent history. The fact is that 166 years ago, or in 1768, the soldiers fired on a crowd of London radicals, leaving a hundred dead and wounded in St. George's Fields, and a Minister said in the House :

There is actual or impending riot in every part of the country. From the tinners of Cornwall to the colliers of Newcastle the spirit of insubordination prevails.

And, except in a few periods, when thousands of the leaders were in jail, that spirit lasted until reforms were granted in the sixth decade of the last century. But I must be brief.

Pitt, cordially supported by the great reformer Wilberforce, crushed the reform-movement, which had very large numbers of followers in all the cities of England, with merciless severity. Thousands went to jail or to Botany Bay. Within less than ten years the " philosophical radicals " rallied the survivors. It is now customary for our comfortable Chestertons to sneer at them, but one would like to see seven men in our time like Jeremy Bentham, Ricardo, Robert Owen, Francis Place, the historian Grote, Sir Francis Burdett, and James Mill: all Atheists. The aristocrat of the group, Burdett (the banker), went to the Tower, and the workers of London attacked it in the hope of releasing him. A few years later they looted the gun-shops and plotted another attack on the British Bastille. Between 1810 and 1820 more thousands went to jail—to vile, fever-sodden dens in which they were herded with the most hardened criminals, of both sexes, without the least regard for sanitation or decency—or to the slavery and brutality of the Australian penal colonies. These were mostly middle-class men and women of comparative refinement. At Manchester the Yeomanry were flung upon a peaceful crowd. But by 1825 the reformers were again active, and they now had the support of such millions of the workers—meetings of 50,000 to 200,000 were held—that the threat of civil war forced the king and Wellington to grant a measure of reform. The people wanted more, and the Chartist Movement began. The meetings—in days without any transport for the workers—now rose to 400,000 in number, and further thousands went to jail, where the terrible conditions drove some to suicide.

I need not go further. What was the attitude of the Church or Churches? You may put it in a word that the Church of England was bitterly hostile and the Methodist Church at the most indifferent; Cobbett, indeed, says that the Methodists were the worst opponents. When the moderate Reform Bill of 1831 came to the House of Lords, after thirty years of struggle and in face of a threat of civil war, of twenty-three bishops twenty-one opposed it. The Archbishop of Canterbury pronounced it " mischievous," and Bishop Horsley said :

I do not know what the mass of the people in any country have to do with the laws but to obey them.

Yet the Bill enfranchised only the middle-class. Apologists now search the records with microscopes to find the name of some obscure parson who advocated reform or to count the religious laymen who helped. They may have that quaint sort of Churchman Cobbett, whose history of the Reformation makes them shudder, but no other leader of any importance.

But there were anti-Christian reformers who thought little of the vote and worked along other lines : education, the reform of the jails, the improvement of the condition of the workers, the emancipation of woman, peace, the abolition of duelling, gambling, and drunkenness, and so on. High above all others in this broad idealism were the great jurist, Jeremy Bentham (who with the historian Grote wrote an explicitly Atheist work which we might do well to reprint), Robert Owen, and Francis Place : all three Atheists. Every reform was advocated by Owen, who spent his fortune in propaganda ; nearly every reform was taken up by Bentham ; and the ablest friend of the workers in their fight to secure combination was Francis Place. Elizabeth Fry (a Quaker) and Howard were conspicuous in the reform of prisons. Lord Brougham (a very doubtful Churchman) worked for the education of the workers.   Joseph Lancaster, Quaker, worked devotedly for the same object.   Lord Shaftesbury, the only prominent Churchman of un-questioned orthodoxy, led a campaign on behalf of many of the workers ; and he strenuously opposed the reform of Parliament, the emancipation of the Jews, the betterment of the lot of the agricultural worker, freedom of the Press, and nearly every other reform.   Like Wilberforce, his heavenly twin in apologetic literature, he confesses in his Diary that he had to barricade his house against the infuriated workers.

If I have any reader who does not appreciate the need of reform, who does not know in what condition the vast majority of the people of England were a hundred years ago, twelve centuries after the introduc-tion of Christianity, I must refer him to the full pic-ture in my *Century of Stupendous Progress.*   Briefly, the political system was grotesque in its corruption to 1832, and very corrupt after that.   The law was gross against the poor and savage in its sentences, while it connived at the universal drunkenness and gambling. Executions were public entertainments ; jails were deadly and indecent ; crime was ten times as rife as it now is.   And the most grievous source of all this and of the almost universal vice (London had 25,000 prostitutes to a million people, according to the police, and unnatural vice and rape were appallingly com-mon), drunkenness, coarseness of manners, mania for fighting (men, women, children, dogs, lions, cocks, etc.), was that the workers were still illiterate to the extent of something like ninety per cent and were exploited like slaves. The average wage was not twelve shillings per week, and the average hours per week for an adult were at least eighty. Children worked ten to twelve hours a day, six days a week, for a penny a day, and were brutalized from early years . . . You remember a once popular picture : Queen Victoria pointing to the Bible and saying : " There is the source of England's greatness."

What did the Church of England do ? Read *The Bishops as Legislators*, by Joseph Clayton, a Churchman, with a preface by the Rev. Stewart Headlam, who calls it a record of " the crimes and follies of the bishops." It is. No bishop supported the Bill for the Prevention of Cruelty to Animals in 1809. Only three attended the House of Lords when, in 1815, a Bill was introduced to Prevent the Use of British Capital in the Slave Trade. They took no part in the discussion of the Prevention of Cruelty to Cattle Bill in 1824. In 1832 fifteen of them were still on the opposition, though even the king was intimidated, to the Parliamentary Reform Bill. Two only voted for the Bill for the Total Suppression of the Slave Trade, and only one or two ever supported the various temperance measures that were introduced from 1839 to 1844. Lord Brougham bluntly said that " only two out of six-and-twenty Right Reverend Prelates will sacrifice their dinner and their regard for their belly . . . to attend and vote." They opposed every measure to relieve the workers. Lord Shaftesbury was so angry when they opposed his one pet proposal that he described them as " timid, time-serving, and great worshippers of wealth and power," and said :

I can scarcely remember an instance in which a clergyman has been found to maintain the cause of labourers in the face of pewholders.

But what, you ask, about Kingsley and Christian Socialism ? They did not appear until the worst fighting was over, in 1850, and broke up in 1855 ; and their real founder, F. D. Maurice, admitted that the aim was to " Christianize Socialism." They did fine work, at a late hour, and Kingsley and Maurice were punished by their Church for it.

What about the Nonconformists, who had " gone back to the pure teaching of Jesus " ? One Methodist minister, Joseph Raynor Stephens, though a Tory, stood out for the people, rather late in the battle ; and he was thrown out of his Church. In the recent book to which I have referred, Dr. Harrison says (p. 53) :

From the churches came the early leaders in the trade union movement and in the co-operative societies ; from them also come the inspiring challenge of the Christian Socialists and the bulk of the men of strong character and personality who led in the high road to reform.

A pity he does not give the names. In ordinary history we read that the right to form trade unions was won, *twenty years before the Christian Socialists appeared,* by Francis Place and his heretical collaborators, and that Robert Owen then dominated the movement for years. As to co-operation, the movement was notoriously inspired by Robert Owen and George Jacob Holyoake, and, though Ludlow and the Christian Socialists rendered it fine service after 1850, it had branches all over the country by that time and the Owenites had familiarized London with the idea long before.

We have now expert sectional histories of the various reform-movements in the first half of the nineteenth century when the fight was most laborious and the reward was obloquy : histories of the trade-union movement, the fight for the liberty of the Press and literature, the emancipation and education of woman, the reform of law and the jails, the establishment of a national system of education, and so on. These are impartial histories by experts. What are the names of the " men (and women) of strong character and personality " who stand out in these histories ? Surely they are Robert Owen, Bentham, Shelley, Burdett, Place, Mill, Grote, Elizabeth Fry, Harriet Martineau, Richard Carlile, Holyoake, Sadler, Brougham, Lancaster, Cobbett, Molesworth, and Leigh Hunt—two Churchmen, one Deist, two Quakers, and the rest Agnostics or Atheists. Not a single clergyman— Stephens was defrocked—appears in the list of honour until the middle of the century ; not a bishop appears until, in the last few decades, the reformers head the big battalions ; not a single Nonconformist or Catholic appears in the first or second rank. In our debate Dr. Harrison claimed that if you search the records carefully you will find Methodist local preachers repeatedly leading local groups. The audience, I regret to say, was quite rude to him at this point. Did anyone ever contend that no Christians ever joined in that heroic struggle of the early nineteenth century ?

Dr. Harrison claimed, in particular, that the Nonconformists rallied to the support of Lancaster and the British and Foreign School Society. Here are the facts. At the beginning of the century, when non-Christian writers like Rousseau, Froebel, and Pestalozzi had already stung Europe to some sense of its shame and the non-Christian Frederic the Great and the French revolutionaries had established systems of national schools, England was still illiterate to the extent of more than ninety per cent. Adam Smith (Deist) had demanded reform a quarter of a century earlier, and every radical echoed the demand. From the Manchester group of radicals two men then set out to do something. Robert Owen founded, at New Lanark, the most wonderful school in Europe and inspired many others. The other man was the Quaker Lancaster who, being a Quaker, would not assent to Owen's ideal of purely secular education, so he started a movement for undenominational schools; and, naturally, the Church folk at once began a rival organization to found Church Schools. Owen, a man of magnificent liberality, gave Lancaster £1,000 and all his support—and the Quakers presently helped to wreck his own enterprise because it was not religious —and gave Bell, the Church leader, £500. The Nonconformists certainly patronized Lancaster's schools; they were the only schools in England their children could attend. In fact, Lancaster, whose schools were desperately poor and cheap, got very wide patronage because he showed the wealthy, as Holman says in his history of education, that " children could be taught next to nothing for next to nothing."

Serious reformers, the men with the broad, full

humanitarian ideal, regarded with some disdain this fight of Bel (Bell) and the Dragon (the Quaker), as the wits called it, and demanded a national system of secular schools. They had to fight for half a century, and both Nonconformists and Church bitterly opposed them. As Adams, the early historian of education, said :

The interdict against a united and national system came from the moral teachers of the people and was pronounced necessary in the interests of religion.

It was 1833 before the Government of this rich and Christianly-elevated country made its first grant for education. It was £20,000, or £50,000 less than the grant for royal stables a few years later. In the same year Prussia spent £600,000 on its schools. In the next seventeen years the government grants amounted to £600,000. All the money was divided between the two religious organizations, the Church getting £475,000. The schooling they gave was atrocious, and the number of children taught was still small. The average weekly pay of a teacher was nine shillings. Yet, in the second half of the nineteenth century, only one in fourteen of the population got any schooling : the proportion was one in six in Prussia, one in seven in Switzerland, one in nine in Holland. As late as 1860 a Government report said that of 2,500,000 children of school-age only 1,500,000 attended any sort of school. So the rising tide of democracy swept away the bishops (whom the Christian Socialists supported in this) and Bel and the Dragon, and got the first national system—fourteen hundred years after Christianity had completed the destruction of the Roman system.

So much for the glorious services in the field of education. Let me glance in conclusion at the women-movement, since our modern preachers find it possible to persuade women that " emancipation " was just a little matter of a vote, because Christianity had secured full justice for women. The idea is preposterous. The nineteenth century found woman in a state of legal, social, and educational, as well as political, subjection from which it has taken a century of fighting to deliver her. Did any clergyman or prominent Churchman (or woman), much less any Church, give any help until, in our own time, women began to quit the churches in millions ? Certainly not. Even Kingsley told her to " Be good, sweet maid," etc. The pioneers in the dark days were Mary Wollstonecraft (Atheist), Fanny Wright (or Mme D'Arusmont, Deist), Harriet Martineau (Atheist), and George Eliot (Atheist), supported by Godwin, Shelley, Owen, Bentham, Holyoake, and J. S. Mill, all Atheists. In America it was Abby Kelly (rebel Quaker), Ernestine Rose (Atheist), Lucretia Mott (rebel Quaker), the Grimkes (Quakers), Mrs. Gage (Atheist), Mrs. Cady Stanton (Atheist), and Miss Susan B. Anthony (Atheist).

In the last year of the century (or about that time) I sat in the lobby of the House of Commons with Mrs. Wolstenholme Elmy (Agnostic) and Mrs. Pankhurst to hear the verdict on the latest Bill for women suffrage—a triennial joke of the House in those days. I seemed to be the only man in sympathy with them.

I worked with them for more than ten years and during the early years never saw a parson in the movement. The Church smiled at them, but not with them. And at last came a great celebration of victory in Hyde Park. I was not invited : but there was a parson on nearly every platform . . . That is the record of Christianity.

CHAPTER X

DO THE CHURCHES HELP TO-DAY?

MANY of my readers who deprecate the slight tincture of irony, if not of scolding, that gets into my ink at times may now be a little more lenient with me. It has, unfortunately, not been possible to include here the full description of English life and character in the first half of the nineteenth century which I have given in other works; and in no other country were life and character higher, while in most Catholic lands they were far lower. But we have seen enough to know that the Europe, which began to fall from the best level of the Greco-Roman civilization in the fourth century, did not rise again to that level until after the middle of the nineteenth. To any man or woman who perceives this it must seem ironic to claim that Christianity made our civilization. The period from the fourth to the nineteenth century was the longest and worst reaction in history; and instead of the barbarians frustrating the civilizing efforts of the Church, the truth is, we saw, that the Church frustrated their efforts to restore civilization, and in the East it degenerated without the least help from barbarians.

Yes, says your up-to-date—more or less up-to-date —apologist, but we do not now claim that Christianity made our civilization ; merely that it made very important contributions. I once, when planning such a work as this (*The Bible in Europe*), got my highly. respectable and esteemed friend Vivian Phelips (who even talks to bishops) to inquire, Jesuitically, of a number of ecclesiastical writers and dignitaries what exactly they do claim ; for I do not write books in order to make a sectarian point but to give people facts about matters of live interest. The reply was that they claim only to have helped or contributed.

So we have examined the contributions. The claim in regard to slavery or of any service to the workers (nine-tenths of the people) is so scandalously opposed to the facts that any responsible writer ought now to be ashamed to mention it. At the most he may say that the Christian insistence on justice must have helped, but the fact is, we saw, that Christendom was sodden with injustice until the nineteenth century. Almost as wildly fictitious is the claim to have elevated woman, taught the world philanthropy, and introduced education. Indeed, seeing what Rome had done in all these matters, and how scandalous is the record of Christendom, we must dismiss all these claims as, at the best, shocking confessions of ignorance of modern social history. The further claims that Christianity introduced a new idea of the sanctity of human life and a higher personal morality are, surely, after all that we have seen about the state of Christendom from the fifth century to the nineteenth, rather humorous.

Apologists seem to proceed on two lines. They use an antiquated historical literature, when they do not simply copy from each other, or they cull pretty flowers from the pages of historians like Lecky and Gibbon who were compelled at their early date to use these older sources. They almost never quote a modern authority on the history of slavery, education, woman, charity, chivalry, etc., when they discuss those subjects. I may claim that I never use any but the latest and best authorities. The other line is to brood over selected passages from the Gospels and Paul, and say that these things *must* have changed the world. Hardly one of them ever makes a serious inquiry whether there was anything new in the moral principles of Paul and the Gospels. If not—and in my *Sources of the Morality of the Gospels* I gave Jewish and pagan parallels for every moral text in the Gospels—there was no reason whatever why they should change the world. Any person who does not suppose that the words (often long sermons or sermonettes) of Jesus were taken down in shorthand and treasured until thirty or forty years later should see that the very composite documents which declare themselves to be " according to Matthew," etc., are just syntheses of the common moral sentiments of the age.

Clerical scholars now perceive, and even some of the most cultivated of them take the line that, while the Stoics entertained a high idealism, they could not influence the world as did a religion that went amongst the people. There seems to be something in apologetic work that destroys a man's sense of proportion and of scientific loyalty. Not only do these scholars fail to read the facts about the position of philoso-

phers in many of the Greek-Roman cities and are prevented by a stupid traditional libel from appreciating
the immense influence of the Epicureans, but they do
not reflect that what was chiefly wanted to remove
the social vices of the Roman world was influence on
monarchs, statesmen, and jurists, not on slaves and
carpenters. They thus close their eyes to the large
and most beneficent influence which the Stoic-
Epicurean ethic or idealism—it was really neither a
philosophy nor a religion—obtained in that world,
and they ignore the account which even Protestant
writers, like Sir Samuel Dill, give of the remarkable
philanthropy that relieved every variety of destitu-
tion in the second century. " What would these
Rationalists do without their Dill ? " one apologist
peevishly exclaimed in the course of a debate with
me. He had himself made the usual copious quotations from Lecky, whose work is half a century older
and now needs careful editing. But we have a dozen
modern writers to quote besides Dill. There is no
dispute about the matter.

However, the answer to all apologists, learned or
otherwise, is that in point of plain historical fact
Christianity did none of the things which it is supposed to have done. There are non-Christians to-day
who profess themselves unable to believe that the
" teaching of Jesus " made no improvement in the
ancient world. These people often still accept as historical the romances about early Church-life and its
saints and martyrs, its communities and catacombs,
which, as I said, even Roman Catholic scholars now
discard, and they repeat uncritically the conventional

cant about the " sublime " teaching of Jesus. It is part of the price we pay for our commercialized journalism and periodical literature. The oracles must be men or women who will " sell," so peeresses and physicists, travellers, and even music-hall performers like Sir H. Lauder, are invited to pen or to broadcast their ideas about Jesus and his " unique " ideas. Not one of them could pass an elementary examination in the religions and philosophies of 1900 years ago and their moral ideals. So the fiction of a " unique " and " sublime " message is maintained.

To the impartial mind the reason for the social sterility of the new religion is clear. Its basic idea—the approaching end of the world—was fatal to any interest in the social order. And even when it became apparent that Jesus was wrong, and the casuists began to explain away his predictions, his ethic was still essentially based upon extremely disputable and, to any educated Greek or Roman, repulsive ideas. Certainly it brought to them a new conception of God ; a God who kept more than half—indeed the great majority of—the race in torture for all eternity. When Paul's theology, of which Jesus was ignorant, was added to this, and the Greeks and Romans further learned that in a fit of temper God had cursed the entire race, because its nudist ancestors had robbed the orchard, the futility of the new ethic was complete. All the Fathers, and especially Augustine, the most influential, and all the more learned doctors for ages, logically drew the conclusion that " the affairs of time " shrank to insignificance in the appalling prospect of our eternal alternatives.

And here is the reply to those who say that the religion and ethic of Jesus have never been tried and we might now begin to try them. By their fruits you shall know them. They were not merely offered to Europe : they were imposed and stamped upon it. And the broad consequences, directly due to the doctrinal framework, were the development of the most mischievous and truculent clerical organization the world had ever seen and the quite general neglect of any ethic at all. Not a tithe of such consequences followed the Atheistic ethic of Kung-fu-tse, and no such consequences—though they were far milder— would have been seen in the Buddhist world if Asia had been faithful to the Atheistic ethic of Gotama. It is worth noting that of four great Asiatic teachers, Gotama, Lao-tse, Kung-fu-tse, and Meng-tse, only the former two had their teaching corrupted in later ages, and these were the only two who wrapped their human ethic in some mysticism.

An ethic established on a mystic basis, whether it is a belief in gods or spirits or the intuitions of philosophers, always will fail. And it never had less chance of success than in our age. The monomark of our age is a note of interrogation. Why ? To tell this world of ours that you must abolish war and poverty because we are all brothers under a heavenly father, when a man must read a whole small library to settle whether there is or is not a heavenly father, and he will have four-fifths of our more learned men against him if he concludes that there is, cannot be regarded as educational service. Whether or no the Christian ethic, as it is in Paul and the Gospels, ought to have produced

rich fruits in the past, it cannot to-day.   The essential bases of it are challenged all over the world.

A type of apologist is appearing who grants the
failure of Christianity during 1800 years, but asks us
to see that the ethic it enshrined or obscured can be
of great service to us.   Let us, he says, bury the past.
That is exactly what I am helping to do.   When even
the majority of Christians use this new language, we
shall no longer expose all the horrors and futilities of
the past.   But the fact is that nine-tenths of them
reject with scorn this position of a few advanced
clerics.   The Churches claim about 60,000,000 members (out of a total population of 160,000,000) in
Great Britain and America.   At least four-fifths of
those are " old-fashioned " Christians : Roman Catholics, the immense majority of the Nonconformists, and
probably the majority of the Anglicans.   They not
only insist on keeping the ethic of Jesus on its old
doctrinal basis, but they firmly believe all the fairy-
tales about what Christianity has done for civilization.   Publications of the Catholic Truth Society,
presumably endorsed by such men as Belloc, Chesterton and Evelyn Waugh, make the claim in all its
Victorian rawness.   So, apparently, do books which
boast of an appeal to 300,000 university students.

That claim is embedded in our national education
and is assumed in the editorial office of nearly every
newspaper in England.   Some of the Churches have
special organizations for seeing that our journalists
and our teachers never venture to question the great
illusion.   To ask us not to recall the social record of
Christianity is as sensible as to ask us not to talk

about war or poverty. We have to continue until the plain lesson of the facts I have here outlined is generally admitted. That plain lesson is that if Europe had been permitted or encouraged by the Church to resume as soon as possible the great cultural work of the Greeks and Romans, as the Ostrogoths and the Lombards wanted, we should to-day be a thousand years further advanced in civilization. If Europe had been permitted and encouraged to cultivate the science which the Arabs and Persians had richly developed by the thirteenth century, we should be five hundred years further advanced to-day. Christianity held the world back, and certainly did not, in compensation, make it chaste and virtuous. For if it had permitted this development of science and free research and discussion, it would have perished long ago.

When we set aside discredited claims, this plain lesson can be obscured only by cutting little areas of light out of the broad darkness of the past and concentrating attention on them. Against any man who said that there have been no good men, no bright areas or periods, between Constantine and the French Revolution that sort of thing might have some educational value. There have been plenty of such good men in 5,000 generations of men and women. We would ask only that the æsthete who likes these things should frankly tell his readers when he is drawing upon ecclesiastical fiction. For instance, he often gives, not only a charming account of Francis of Assisi, but an attractive picture of his followers, the bare-footed friars. In point of fact, his Order was corrupt and convulsed with quarrels within thirty years. No reform of the monasteries ever lasted a century. In the same way we get quite unhistorical and misleading accounts of the cathedral-builders, the Christian knights, the crusades, Roger Bacon, Luther, the Counter-Reformation, and hundreds of other things. There is dire need of a Rationalist Encyclopædia.

Suppose we could forget, suppose we were permitted to forget, all this malodorous past with its crimes and follies and waste, how should we confront the Churches of our time? Some imagine us as Rationalist bulls to whom Church, Christianity, Jesus, and religion are red rags. On the contrary, in our coldest and most dispassionate moods we are just as emphatically opposed to them. It would be a poor type of man or woman who, knowing all the facts of which I have given a selection and a summary, did not feel some warmth of resentment when he reflects that those vices and cruelties from which the nineteenth century partially relieved our civilization might, but for Christian tyranny and misdirection, have been removed centuries ago. But let us by all means be cold, intellectual, scientific.

We live in an age of such problems and perplexities that we will welcome all the intellectual light and all the genuine idealist sentiment we can obtain. But our perplexities are social. It is loose and flabby thinking that asks us not to criticize the Churches because they " do good " in the personal sense. Not only has the standard of personal character risen considerably during the hundred years in which church-going

or Bible-reading has shrunk by two-thirds, not only
is the three-fourths majority of this nation which
(according to clerical statistics) never goes to Church
no different in character from the one-fourth that for
one reason or other does, but common sense, to say
nothing of science, asks, when you say that an agency
does good, whether it is the best agency for the purpose, whether it is keeping out of action some more
effective agency. The Churches certainly are. It is
because our journalism, literature, and education sustain this convention that they are the nation's one
source of inspiration that we rear each new generation
in the sloppy, chaotic, ineffectual way that we do.
The new science of social psychology interprets what
we call character as a social product, and points out
that by a comprehensive scientific operation, embrac-
ing the work of the physiologist and psychologist as
well as what we call the educationist, we could make
enormously more progress than ever. The Churches
would fight such a proposal as they once fought evolution : it denies that men have " souls." It is nothing
to them that three-fourths of us already, on their own
statistical confession, never come under their influence and do not care two pins what was said in Judæa
two thousand years ago. So we are left to draw our
rules and inspiration from life itself, as men in the
best ages always have done. We want to substitute
a national and international scientific organization for
this casual, haphazard, take-it-or-leave-it business.

As to our social perplexities, the new Christianity
has proved as barren as the old. Some of us have
watched the Churches for fifty years catching-up with

humanitarian movements. The records of Church conferences during the last few decades are full of warnings that unless the Church takes up this or that cause or movement it is going to be left stranded on the beach when the idealist tide moves on. For ten years I have worked mainly for American readers and watched American religious life. During the last five years it has been amusing. Down to 1930 the pulpit-theme was that Hoover was the God-sent man, and the stupendous national prosperity was God's reward for the virtue of His people. Came the depression, and from pulpit after pulpit it was preached that people must thank God that material prosperity no longer filmed their souls and implore Him never to restore the curse. Came Roosevelt, the real God-sent man, and the golden hope of a renewal of prosperity ; mingled with acute disappointment that he included no interpreters of the Christian ethic in his Brain Trust. America smiles. The men all over the world who confront our problems never consult the Churches; though the American Churches have very elaborate social bureaux and social experts and representatives at Washington.

So it is in every country, on every problem. The Pope, despite his intrigues, was kept out of the League of Nations. Mr. Macdonald, in all his new piety, does not consult the Archbishop. Dr. Norwood (quoted recently in the *Literary Guide*) says in his *Indiscretions of a Preacher* (1932, p. 187) :

The Church has a well-established bias toward charity and the succouring of the unfortunate, but no one takes her seriously as the protagonist of a better world-order.

Naturally : because we outsiders taught her all she knows about a better world-order. It was only when the majority of us were convinced that war is evil, that the poor must be uplifted, and so on, that the Churches discovered that the ethic of Jesus implied these things. That is called " sneering at religion." It is a simple statement of historical facts.

And even now the Churches have no definite and consistent message. The nearest approach to one is the condemnation of all war. But will the Churches all join the C.O.'s if a defensive war is forced upon us ? One does not, happily, see them asking us to relax our arms while all the world continues armed. In other words, they will behave in each country as they did in 1914. One would say that moral principle was more plainly needed in discussing the distribution of wealth, for we all loathe war and would like to see how we can get rid of it. But is there a single Church that dare talk more than vague platitude about it ? The Pope co-operates with Socialism in Belgium—even wanted at first, if his terms were granted, to co-operate with the Soviet authorities—and also co-operates with Mussolini. He openly comes to terms with the Spanish Republic, and secretly encourages Gil Robles to attempt to strangle it. A priest in Detroit thunders against the banks and capitalists, and in New York the Church is their friend. Are the Protestant Churches different ? They inculcate justice ; and they leave it to the individual to say what precisely is just.

All this is futile, distracting, unworthy of a scientific age. In school-museums of the future one of the exhibits that will most entertain the children will be a model of a church with rows of grown-up men and women sitting solemnly while some peculiarly-dressed person urges them to be good. It is an anachronism. It survives only because the Churches are to-day mainly economic corporations which fight for survival. Does it matter ? That is what advanced people were asking, with a superior air, a few years ago in Rome, Vienna, and Madrid. Now, somehow, the advanced movements are in the mud. At all events, we may insist on two things. First, these economic corporations which profess to teach us to be just, truthful, and honourable shall themselves be just, truthful, and honourable in their appeals. Secondly, however long they survive and however many million people cling to them, the scientific organization of life shall not be represented as superfluous because Salvation Armies can show a few converted drunkards or burglars in their annual reports. Life is now too pregnant with possibilities to be left to these heavy night-watchmen of the Middle Ages.

THE LIES and FALLACIES of the ENCYCLOPEDIA BRITANNICA

of the

ENCYCLOPEDIA BRITANNICA

HOW POWERFUL AND SHAMELESS CLERICAL FORCES
CASTRATED A FAMOUS WORK OF REFERENCE

---

by
JOSEPH McCABE

THE POPE'S EUNUCHS

A few years ago I had occasion to refer in one of my books to the male soprani of the papal chapel at Rome. These castrated males, sexually mutilated, as every priest and every Italian knew, for soprani in the choir of the Sistine Chapel, were the amusement of Rome when it developed a large degree of skepticism but a grave scandal to the American and British Catholics who began to arrive about the middle of the last century. One of the vices which the Spaniards had brought to Italy in the 16th century along with the Borgia family and the Spanish Roman Emperors was the falsetto singer. There were artists who could sing falsetto with distinction, but as the opera gained in popularity in Italy the practice began of emasculating boys with good voices and retaining them as male soprani or, as the Italians, with their usual lack of Christian reticence about sex called them, the *castrati*. They were in every opera in the 18th century, but foreign visitors were never reconciled to them. The famous English weekly, *The Spectator*, wrote about "the shrill celestial whine of eunuchs," and by the end of the 18th century they began to fade out of the opera-house.

But, as the word "celestial" indicates, they were found also in the choir of all churches that were proud of their music, particularly in the chapel of the Vatican Palace, the Sistine Chapel, one of the greatest shrines of art as well as of virtue and piety in Rome. And the churches clung to their eunuchs when public opinion almost drove them out of opera. The plea seems to have been that there was some indelicacy, or risk of it, in having females in the church choir, so the priests chose to ignore the rather indelicate nature of the operation of emasculation. The fact was as well known as the celibacy of the clergy. Grove's standard "Dictionary of Music and Musicians" (1927) says in a section titled "Castrati":

> "Eunuchs were in vogue as singers until comparatively recent times; they were employed in the choirs of Rome."

So Macmillan's and all other leading dictionaries of music, and English and American visitors to Rome before 1870 who wrote books rarely failed to mention, with smirks of humor or frowns of piety, how the beautiful music of the papal choir was due in large part to manufactured soprani. In the later years of the last century I talked with elderly men who had, out of curiosity, dined or lunched with these quaint servants of God.

An American reader wrote me that a Catholic friend, who had doubtless, as is usual, consulted his pastor, indignantly denied the statement. It was one of the usual "lies of Freethinkers." For an easily accessible authority, reliable on such a point, I referred him to the Encyclopedia Britannica. In all editions to 1928 the article "Eunuchs," after discussing the barbaric African custom of making eunuchs for the harem, said:

> "Even more vile, as being practiced by a civilized European nation, was the Italian practice of castrating boys to prevent the natural development of the voice, in order to train them as adult soprano singers, such as might formerly be found in the Sistine Chapel. Though such mutilation is a crime punishable with severity, the supply of soprani never failed as long as these musical powers were in demand in high quarters. Driven long ago from the Italian stage by public opinion they remained the musical glory and the

moral shame of the papal choir till the accession of Pope Leo XII, one of whose first acts was to get rid of them." ·

My correspondent replied, to my astonishment, that there was no such passage in the Britannica, and I began the investigation of which I give the results in the present little book. I found at once that in the 14th edition, which was published in 1929, the passage had been scandalously mutilated, the facts about church choirs suppressed, and the reader given an entirely false impression of the work of Leo XII. In this new edition the 'whole of the above passage is cut out and this replaces it:

"The Italian practice of castrating boys in order to train them as adult soprano singers ended with the accession of Pope Leo XIII." ·

The reader is thus given to understand that the zealous Pope found the shameless practice lingering in the opera-houses and forbade it. The fact, in particular, that the Church of Rome had until the year 1878 not only permitted this gross mutilation but required it for the purpose of its most sacred chapel—that Pope Pius IX, the first Pope to be declared infallible by the Church, the only modern Pope for whom the first official stage of canonization was demanded, sat solemnly on his throne in the Sistine Chapel for 20 years listening to "the shrill celestial whine of eunuchs"—were deliberately suppressed. Those facts are so glaringly inconsistent with the claims of Catholic writers in America that the suppression was clearly due to clerical influence, and I looked for the method in which it had been applied.

The Encyclopedia is, as its name implies, an ancient British institution inspired by the great French Encyclopedia of the 18th century. As the American reading public increased it served both countries, and by 1920 the special needs of American readers and the great development of science and technics made it necessary to prepare an entirely recast edition. It now had an American as well as a British staff and publishing house, and it was dedicated to King George and President Hoover. The last trace of the idealism of its earlier publishers disappeared. What bargains were secretly made to secure a large circulation we do not know but when the work was completed in 1928 the Westminster Catholic Federation, which corresponds to the Catholic Welfare organization in America, made this boast in its annual report:

The revision of the Encyclopedia Britannica was undertaken with a view to eliminate matter which was objectionable from a Catholic point of view and to insert what was accurate and unbiased. The whole of the 28 volumes were examined, objectionable parts noted, and the reasons for their deletion or amendment given. There is every reason to hope that the new edition of the Britannica will be found very much more accurate and impartial than its predecessors."

This blazing indiscretion seems to have struck sparks in the publishing offices at London and New York—later reprints of this emasculated edition have the imprint of "The University of Chicago," which seems to have taken over the responsibility—for on August 9, 1929, a singular public notice appeared in what is called the Agony Column of the London *Times*. I should explain to American readers that the first page of this famous paper is given up to advertisements and public and private notices and the two central columns are so much used by separated and broken-hearted lovers ("Ethel. Where are you? I suffer agony for you. Your adoring George," etc.) and ladies who have lost their pets or are in need of money etc., that many frivolous folk take the paper for the humor of those two columns. One of the longest notices that ever appeared in it was that of August 9. It runs:

"Westminster Catholic Federation (in large type). On behalf of the Westminster Catholic Federation we desire to state that it has been brought to our attention that the wording of the second paragraph of the report of the Vigilance Sub-Committee of the Federation, (page 18 of the Federation's 21st Annual Report) concerning the forthcoming edition of the Encyclopedia Britannica has apparently given rise to a misunderstanding. We therefore wish to make it clear that it was far from our intention in the above-mentioned report to suggest that the Federation has exercised any influence whatever upon the editing of the Encyclopedia. Such a suggestion would be devoid of any vestige of foundation. The facts are that the Federation offered to the Editor of the Encyclopedia its assistance in checking statements of fact appearing in articles in the previous edition dealing with the Catholic Church in its historical, doctrinal, or theological aspects. This offer was accepted, and the Federation was thus enabled to draw attention to *certain errors of date and other facts regarding the teaching and discipline of the Catholic Church. Beyond this the Federation has had no hand whatever in the preparation or editing of articles for the new edition of the Encyclopedia Britannica on whatever subject,* and any suggestions to the contrary is, as we have said, without the slightest foundation.

A.J., London, W.C.2."

I have italiziced the essential part of this singular message so that the reader will bear in mind that Catholic authorities gave the public their solemn assurance that they had requested—demanded might be a better word—only alterations of wrong dates and statements about the teaching and discipline of the Church.

Penitence is a familiar and beautiful practice in the Catholic world but we common folk like to have truth even in penitence. The example I have already given of the suppression of material facts and a natural comment on them in regard to eunuch singers and ine entirely false impression conveyed by the sentences which Catholics supplied gives the lie at once to this apology. Undisputed facts which are strictly relevant to an examination of Catholic claims have been suppressed. They have nothing to do with dates or the teaching and discipline of the Church. It is an axiom of Catholic moral theology that "suppression of the truth is a suggestion of untruth," and the substituted passage goes beyond this. I propose to show that this introduction of a painfully familiar Catholic policy has been carried right through the Encyclopedia. Naturally the immense majority of its articles do not in any way relate to the church, and I do not claim that I have compared every short notice or every sentence in longer articles, in the 11th and 14th editions of the Britannica. Even these short unsigned notices, referring to such matters as popes and saints, have often been falsified, and I give a few examples. But I am mainly concerned with important alterations. There are still passages in the Encyclopedia which the Catholic clergy do not like. Writers who are still alive may have objected to the adulteration of their work, or the facts may be too notorious for the editors to permit interference. But I give here a mass of evidence of the corrupt use of the great power which the Catholic Church now has: a warning what the public may expect now that that Church has, through its wealth and numbers, secured this pernicious influence on publications, the press, the radio, and to an increasing extent on education and even the cinema.

CASTRATING THE ENCYCLOPEDIA

It will be useful to give first the outcome of a somewhat cursory survey, page by page, of the first few volumes of the Encyclopedia. More important—in their bearing on the Church—articles in later volumes commonly have the initial X at the close, which seems to be the cloak of the Catholic adulterator. This will enable any reader to compare for himself passages in the 11th and the 14th editions, but the conspirator shows his hand even in large numbers of short unsigned, especially biographical, notices. It is, of course, understood that the work had to be considerably abbreviated to accommodate new developments of science and life, in the 14th edition, but when you find that the curtailing consists in suppressing an unpleasant judgment or a fact about a Pope while unimportant statements of fact are untouched, and when you find the life of a saintly man or the flattering appreciation of his work little affected while the life or work of a heretic is sacrificed, you have a just suspicion.

An example is encountered early in the first volume in the short notices of the Popes Adrian I and Adrian II. Adrian was the Pope of Charlemagne's time, and every historian knows that the emperor came, as he shows in his letters, to despise the Pope and to defy him on a point of doctrine; for at that time the use and veneration of statues in the churches was made a doctrinal issue between East and West. The notice of Adrian in the older edition of the Encyclopedia was one of those inexpert paragraphs by some man who knew nothing about the importance of the quarrel, but a priestly hand has untruthfully inserted in the new edition:

"The friendly relations between Pope and Emperor were not disturbed by the difference which arose between them on the question of the veneration of images."

Here, instead of abbreviating, the editor gratuitously inserts new matter, and it is untruthful. The Pope, whose safety depended upon the favor of Charlemagne, said little, it is true, but at a time when "the veneration of images"—as historians persist in calling statues— was the greatest issue in the Church, Charlemagne put his own name to a book in which Roman practice and theory were denounced as sinful, the whole Gallican Church was got to support him, and the timid protests of the Pope were contemptuously ignored.

The touch in the notice of Pope Adrian II has just as little to do with dates and discipline and is just the suppression of a fact which the Church does not like. The real interest of the Pope is that he presided over the Church in the latter part of the 9th century, the time when it was sinking into its deepest degradation. The appalling coarseness of life is seen in the fact that the Pope's daughter was abducted by the son of a bishop and brother of a leading cardinal, and when the Pope got the Emperor to send troops, he murdered them. The notice of the Pope in the 11th edition adds that "his (the noble abductor) reputation suffered but a momentary eclipse," which is perfectly true, for the abducting family were high both in church and nobility and the Romans in large part supported them. But the sentence has been cut out of the new edition. Little touches of that sort, not always condensing the text but always—and generally untruthfully—in the interest of the Church occur repeatedly.

Such articles as "Agnosticism" and "Atheism" did not concern the Catholic Church in particular and were left to more honest but hardly less bigoted clerical writers. I need say of them only that they reflect the cloudy ideas of some theologian and tell the reader no more about the situation in these matters today than if they had been written by a Hindu swami. A different procedure is found when we come to "Alban." The old notice said that he is usually styled "the proto-martyr of Britain," and added "but it is impossible to determine with certainty whether he ever existed, as no mention of him occurs till the middle of the 6th century"; which is correct. But these zealots for correctness of dates and discipline have, in the new edition, turned him into an indisputably real saint and martyr. He is now "the first martyr of Britain" and all hints of dispute about his historicity are cut out.

We pass to "Albertus Magnus"—why an Encyclopedia in English should not say Albert the Great is not explained; possibly the epithet is less offensive to the eye in Latin—and this article is condensed (as the whole new editions had to be) in a peculiarly clerical manner. The original writer had never properly informed the reader that Albert was so much indebted to Aristotle for his "science" that he was known to Catholic contemporaries as "the Ape of Aristotle" and that he was apt to be so inaccurate that he described Plato (who lived a century before the Stoic school was founded) as a Stoic. These things are sacrificed in the sacred cause of abbreviation but new compliments, such as that Bacon called Albert "the most noted of Christian philosophers" are inserted to fill the gaps.

The article "Albigensians" is one in which a modern student would most surely expect a modern encyclopedia to replace the conventional old article by one in line with our historical knowledge. Instead of this we get a page article reduced to half a page, and this is done chiefly by cutting out 25 lines in which the older writer had honestly explained that the Pope turned the brutal Knights of France upon the Albigensians only when 20 years preaching failed to make the least impression on them and 10 lines showing what "vast inquests" of the Inquisition were still needed after years of slaughter by the Pope's savage "crusaders." We therefore recognize the anointed hand of the abbreviator. And it is clear that the editor or sub-editor cheated the public of a most important truth by entrusting this article to Catholic "correctors of dates and discipline." We now fully realize the importance from the angle of the history of civilization of this brilliant but anti-Christian little civilization in the South of France (close to Arab Spain) and what Europe lost. Of the brutality of the massacre and the Pope's dishonesty in engineering it the reader is, of course, given no idea, though these are found in the Pope's extant letters.

Even such articles as that on "Alembert"—the famous French skeptic and scientist D'Alembert—seem to have been handed over to the clerical shearer, for the proper appreciation of his character and ability and his work against the Jesuits are the chief material that has been abbreviated, but we turn with more interest to the "Alexander" Popes. I need not say that anybody who expects an up-to-date account of the great Alexandrian schools of science and of the splendor of life under the early Ptolemies will be deeply disappointed, but it is chiefly the name of Pope Alexander VI which here catches the eye.

Catholics long ago abandoned their attempts to whitewash the historical figure of that amazingly erotic and unscrupulous Spaniard and especially after the work of the Catholic historian Dr. L. Pastor it is impossible to suggest outside the Sunday School that there has been any libelling of this Pope. What the clerical retouchers have mainly done is to remove sentences in which the older writer correctly, though only casually and incidentally, let the reader know that such a Pope was possible only because the Church was then extraordinarily corrupt. He admitted, for instance, that Alexander had been notoriously corrupt for years, as a cardinal, when he was elected Pope:

"Although ecclesiastical corruption was then at its height his riotous mode of life called down upon him a very severe reprimand from Pope Pius II."

This is cut out, of course, though we still have the letter in which the Pope—himself a rake in his early years, by the way—describes the cardinal's scandalous life. Cut out also (for abbreviation) is this passage:

"A characteristic instance of the corruption of the papal court is the fact that Borgia's daughter Lucrezia lived with his mistress Giulia, who bore him a daughter, Laura, in 1492 (the year of his consecration as Pope)."

In short, while it would have elicited the scorn of historians to attempt to suppress all mention of Alexander's mistresses and children the article of the 11th edition, which was correct as far as it went, is so manipulated that the reader has no idea that the Cardinal was

7

brazen in his conduct at the actual time of his election and entertained his mistress, who was painted on one of the walls of the Vatican Palace as the Virgin Mary, and his children in the "Sacred Palace"; and that this was due to the general sordid corruption of the Church. Sexual looseness was the least pernicious of Borgia's vices, but where the old article noticed that his foreign policy was inspired only by concern to enrich his children and "for this object he was ready to commit any crime and to plunge all Italy into war," this Catholic stickler for accuracy has cut it out.

Soon after Alexander we come to Antonelli. This man was Cardinal Secretary of State to Pope Gregory XVI and Pope Pius IX, who is counted a saint by American Catholics. He was the son of a poor wood-cutter and he died a millionaire: he left $20,000,000—leaving a bastard daughter, a countess, to fight greedy relatives for it. He had refused to take priestly orders because he wanted freedom. His greed, looseness, and complete indifference to the vile condition of the Papal States were known to everybody. In the 11th edition we read of him:

"At Antonelli's death the Vatican finances were found to be in disorder, with a deficit of 45,000,000 lire. His personal fortune, accumulated during office, was considerable and was bequeathed almost entirely to his family. . . . His activity was directed almost exclusively to the struggle between the Papacy and the Italian *Risorgimento*, the history of which is comprehensible only when the influence exercised by his unscrupulous grasping and sinister personality is fully taken into account."

The last part of this now reads "is comprehensible only when his unscrupulous influence is fully taken into account." Apart from the one word "unscrupulous" the reader is totally misled as to his character.

The article on Aquinas was already written favorably to the Church and only a few light touches were needed. But the eagle eye caught a sentence, perfectly accurate but offensive to Catholics, in the short notice of the noblest figure of the 12th century, Arnold of Brescia. It said:

"At the request of the Pope he was seized by order of the Emperor . . . and hanged."

Out goes the reference to the Pope, who had tried for years to catch Arnold before he acted on a perjured passport from the Emperor; and no idea is given of the remarkable position of the premature democrat in the history of European thought.

More amusing is the manipulation of the notice of "Arthur" of Britain. In the 11th edition he is frankly presented to the reader as a myth, as the popular conception of him certainly is. All that we can say with any confidence is that there seems to have been a sort of captain named Arthur in the ragged military service of one of the half-civilized and wholly brutal British "kings" after the departure of the Romans. In this new compendium of modern scholarship (now sponsored by the University of Chicago) Arthur has been converted into an undisputed and highly respectable reality; a "King of Britain" who led his Christian armies against the pagan Anglo-Saxons. And this is done on the authority of a monk who wrote two and a half centuries later! There is no proof that this fine achievement is due to the Catholic Federation, but just as detectives look for the trade-mark of a particular burglar when a bank has been robbed. . . .

"Athanasius, Bishop of Alexandria" becomes, by the same process "Athanasius the Great, saint, and bishop of Alexandria," and so important to us moderns that, in spite of the needs of space for new thought, the long article (by a cleric), is lengthened in the new edition. The short article on Atheism, which follows closely upon it, is, as I said, quite worthless. A British royal chaplain writes on it as if it were a point in dispute in some Pacific Island, instead of a burning

8

question of our time. He seems to have been totally unaware of, or indifferent to, the fact that a few years earlier the majority of American scientists had (in Leuba) declared themselves Atheists, and that in the seven years before he wrote his article tens of millions of folk, from Annam across Europe to Chile, had abandoned the churches to embrace Atheism. Naturally a learned staff which announces in the preface to the Encyclopedia that it considers that the wicked materialistic philosophy of the 19th century has been slain by the new science thinks such things beneath its notice.

Early in the B's we get the same light touches of the clerical brush. The long and appreciative article on the great jurist and Atheist Jeremy Bentham—that he was an outspoken Atheist is, of course, not stated—one of the most powerful idealists of the post-Napoleonic period, is mercilessly cut, while the old notices of the insignificant Pope Benedicts remain. At least, I notice only one cut. It is said in the old article that Benedict IX, perhaps the vilest man who ever wore the tiara—his almost immediate successor spoke of his "rapes, murders, and other unspeakable acts"—appears to have died inpenitent." That is cut out. It saves so much space.

A long article is inserted in the new edition on "Birth Control": a subject that had no article in the old edition. This consists of the findings of a series of conferences on the subject mostly overshadowed by church influence. These fill several pages while the elementary grounds for seeing the necessity of it—the rapid multiplication of population in modern times—are barely noticed. A section on the religious attitude is written by the Rev. Sir James Marchant, a parson of the Church of England who is fanatically Catholic in sex-matters. It begins with the plump untruth that "it is now recognized that the objections on religious grounds to birth control must be fully heard," and it consists mainly of a sort of sermon by the Cardinal Archbishop of Westminster, whose views are "shared by many other religious communities." We should like to hear of one which as a body has condemned birth control. Then the mysterious X appears at last with a tendentious summary of the whole article—against birth control. Strange stuff for a modern encyclopedia.

Even the article on Bismarck is retouched, mainly in the section which describes his great struggle with the Catholics of Germany, and the article "Body and Mind" is as modern as the Athanasian Creed. No evidence appears that this new article, so profoundly important in view of the advanced condition of American psychology—four manuals out of five refuse to admit "mind"—was written by a Catholic, so I will be content to say that it is an affront to American science. Later appears another new article "Bolshevism." But there was, naturally, no article with that title in the 11th edition so that the Catholic censor knew nothing about it until it appeared in print. Its accuracy and coldness must have pained him. It is written by Professor Laski.

I say the Catholic censor but there was obviously team-work on both sides of the Atlantic, though Gildea is the only sophist mentioned on the American side. And the next item to catch the clerical eye and raise the clerical blood-pressure was the fair article on "Giordano Bruno," in the 11th edition. You can almost see the fury with which the three columns are reduced to less than a column in the 14th edition, and this is done by cutting out about 100 lines of sober appreciation of the great ex-monk and scholar's ability and character. Cutting out flowers is not enough. A new paragraph informs the innocent reader:

"Apart from his disdainful, boasting nature and his attack on contemporary Christianity, the chief causes of Bruno's downfall were his rejection of the Aristotelic astronomy for the Copernican . . . and his pantheistic tendencies."

The undisputed truth is that he was burned alive by the Papacy, which came to a corrupt agreement with the Venetians in order to get hold of him and satisfy its bitter hatred of the critic.

9   ENCYCLOPEDIA BRITANNICA

"Buddha and Buddhism" are mangled in the new edition in the most extraordinary fashion. Twelve pages of sound, useful matter are cut down to three; as if Buddhism had meantime died in the East and ceased to be of any interest to westerners. Between the publication of the two editions of the Encyclopedia a good deal has been written on the creed of Buddha, and it is quite generally agreed by experts on the religion or on India that he was an Atheist. Not a single word is said about the question, and the reader is left at the mercy of every pamphleteer who talks about the "religious genius" of the man.

More definitely and recognizably Catholic is the tampering with the notice of St. Catherine. There are two saints of that name, Catherine of Alexandria and Catherine of Siena, and the 11th edition rightly said:

"Of the former history has *nothing* to tell . . . that St. Catherine actually existed there is no evidence to disprove, and it is possible that some of the elements in her legend are due to confusion with the story of Hypatia."

This was moderate enough. We do not have to "disprove" the existence of martyrs, and the supposed evidence in favor of her historicity is now rejected even by some Catholic experts on martyrs, while the details are often comical and the general idea is certainly based upon Hypatia. Yet in this severely-examined and up-to-date compendium of knowledge we find the first sentence of the above changed to: Of St. Catherine of Alexandria history has *little* to tell." The rest is cut out and, we are brazenly told that "her actual existence is generally admitted." The article on Catherine of Siena was already inaccurately favorable to Catholic claims in the 11th edition, so it is allowed to stand. The masterful Siennese nun had nothing like the political influence ascribed to her, and it was not she but the threats of the Romans that brought the Popes back from Avignon to Rome.

In the article "Church History," to which in the new edition, the ominous X is appended, there are just slight changes here and there in the generally orthodox article. The treatment is as far removed from modern thought as Alaska is from Florida. It is much the same with the string of Popes who had the name Clement. The reader is still not told that many historians refuse to admit "Clement I" as the first of the Popes—he is completely ignored in the Letter of the Romans to the Corinthians of the year 96 A.D. and many of the other Clements, who were notoriously of disreputable character, are discreetly retouched, though the earlier notices let them off lightly. Clement V, a French adventurer, who sold himself to the French King on vile conditions in order to get the Papacy, has the words "in pursuance of the King's wish he summoned the Council of Vienne" (to hold a trial of the monstrous vices of his predecessor and the still more scandalous vices of the Knights Templar, as we shall see) changed to: "Fearing that the state would proceed independently against the alleged heresies he summoned the Council of Vienne"; which is one sort of abbreviation and leaves the reader entirely ignorant of the character of the Pope. Clement VI, a notoriously sensuous and dissipated man, is left in his Catholic robes. Of Clement VII the earlier edition said: "Though free from the grosser vices of his predecessors he was a man of narrow outlook and interests." The whole of this is cut out, suppressing both his vices and those of his predecessors. Clement XIV is said to have suppressed the Jesuits only because he thought it necessary for the peace of the Church. This is a familiar Jesuit claim and an audacious lie. In the bull of condemnation Clement endorses all the charges against the Jesuits.

The article "Conclave" sounds like one that was ripe for the shearer, but even in the 11th edition it was written by a priest. And it had a Jesuit touch that the censor is careful not to correct. As the leading authority it names a Catholic work which, in any case, few have any chance to consult, while it does not mention the standard history of Papal Conclaves, that of Petrucelli della Gattina (four volumes of amazing disclosures), of which there is now an English version (V. Petrie's "Triple Crown," 1935). But of little tricks of this kind, especially in pressing "sound" authorities upon the reader and concealing from him that there are good critical works that he ought to read, there is so much that it would be tiresome to trace it all. We will consider larger matters.

THE TAMING OF HISTORY

The short and worthless note under "Chivalry" in the old En-cyclopedia would in any new edition that frankly aimed to give the reader summaries of modern knowledge have been replaced by some account of the present general agreement of historians that the alleged Age of Chivalry (110-1400 A.D.) is sheer myth. No leading historical expert on France, Germany, England, Italy, or Spain during that period recognizes it. They all describe such a generally sordid character in the class of knights and nobles, particularly in what are considered by ro-mantic writers the specific virtues of chivalry—chastity and the zeal for justice—that the student of general history feels justified in con-cluding that, on our modern idea of chivalry, this was precisely the most unchivalrous section of civilized history. Of this truth not a syllable is given, not even a hint that the myth is questioned. So editors, moral essayists and preachers, who take their history from the Encyclopedia, continue to shame our age with reminders of the glorious virtues of the later Middle Ages. However, we will return to this when we come to "Knighthood" and " Troubadours" where we shall find a little more satisfaction.

The article on "Confucius" in the 11th edition was written by a Protestant missionary, Dr. Legge, and he was not only a fine scholar of Chinese but a singularly honest type of missionary. In the 14th edition his excellent five pages are cut to three. One recognizes the need for abbreviation, though when one finds a four-page article on Falconry, which is really rather rare today, 16 pages on football, etc., one feels that the work of condensing might have been done differently. However in the case of a great Atheist like Confucius an Encyclopedia that would please the clergy must not pay too many compliments, and the Catholic X, who probably knows as little about Chinese as about biochemistry valiantly cuts the work of the expert to three pages, adding his X to Legge's initials at the foot. One illustration of the way in which it is done will suffice. Confucius so notoriously rejected belief in gods and spirits that Legge's statement of this has to remain. But there is one point on which Christians hold out desperately. Legge told the truth about it, and X cuts it out.

It is whether Confucius anticipated Christ by many centuries in formulating the Golden Rule, or, to meet the better-informed apologists, whether Confucius recommended it only in a negative form. As nothing is more common, and probably has been since the Stone Age, than to hear folk say, "Do as you would be done by," or some such phrase, which is the Golden rule in fireside English, the fuss about it is amusing. How-ever, the champions of Christ's unique moral genius will have it that Confucius gave it only in the negative form. "What you do not like when done to yourself do not do to others." As the Christian decalogue consists almost entirely of negations, that is not bad. But in the 11th edition Legge goes on to explain that when a disciple asked the master of it could be expressed in a word he used a compound Chinese word which means "As Heart" ..or Reciprocity), and Legge says that he conceived the rule in its most positive and most comprehensive form. The Rev. Mr. X suppresses this to save space and inserts this pointless sentence:

"It has been said that he only gave the rule in a negative form to give force to a positive statement."

So the preacher and pamphleteer continue to inform folk on the authority of J. Legge in the Encyclopedia Britannica that Confucius knew the Golden Rule only in the inferior negative form.

There was no need to let X loose with his little hatchet upon the article "Constantine." It was, like "Charlemagne," "Justinian," and most such articles, already subservient to piety and an outrage on historical truth. Constantine's character is falsified by suppressing facts. For instance, in profane (and ancient Roman) history you will read that Constantine was driven from Rome by the scorn of the Romans because he had had his wife and his son murdered, probably in a fit of jealousy. Here his quitting Rome and founding Constantinople is represented as a matter of high strategy and a care for the interests of religion. Not a hint about the "execution" of his wife, bastard son, and nephew. The Romans compared him to Nero.

In 20 pages on "Crime" we do not get any statistical information whatever about the relation of crime to religious education, which after all is of some interest to our age, so, skipping a few minor matters, we come to "Crusades." Again the article in the old Encyclopedia was so devout and misleading that X could not improve upon it. It admits that Europe had become rather boorish owing to the barbaric invasions but claims that it did provide the Church with the grand force of knighthood to use against the wicked Moslem:

"The institution of chivalry represents such a clerical consecration, for ideal ends and noble purposes, of the martial impulses which the Church had endeavored to check. . . ."

And so on. A lie in every syllable. The knights of Europe were, with rare exceptions, erotic brutes—their ladies as bad—as all authoritative historians describe them. The Pope—his words are preserved—dangled the loot of the highly civilized East before their eyes in summoning the first Crusade; and the story, almost from begining to end, is a mixture of superstition, greed, and savagery. The only faint reference to the modern debunking of the traditional fairy tale is:

"When all is said the Crusades remain a wonderful and perpetually astonishing act in the great drama of human life."

Even a cleric must be 150 years old and ignorant of history to write honestly like this article.

Pope "Saint" Damasus I retains his nimbus in the new great Encyclopedia though he is now known to have been an unscrupulous Spanish adventurer and, as contemporary priests said, "tickler of matrons' ears." A few remarks that were made in the short article in the 11th edition about the incredible massacres at his election and the impeachment of him later (for adultery) in the civil court are cut out. But while "Damasus" is abbreviated thus by cutting out references to his misdeeds, the article "Darwin," is shortened by suppressing whole paragraphs of Professor Poulton's fine appreciation of his character and work and the world-honors he received. "David" is in this modern Encyclopedia treated as much more important than Darwin, and, while even theologians now often reject him as a myth or a dim shapeless figure, almost the whole biblical account of him is given as history.

But I have overlooked the short article on the "Dark Age," which is nauseous. There was no article in the 11th edition on it, so an obscure professor at a third-rate British University has been commissioned to write one. The phrase was, he says, "formerly used to cover the whole period between the end of the classical civilization and the revival of learning in the 15th century." Bunk. No historian extended it beyond the end of the 11th century. In short, he copies certain American professors of history who cater to Catholics and who give no evidence that they can even read medieval literature. The period is only dark "owing to the insufficiency of the historical evidence" yet "great intellectual

12

work was done in unfavorable conditions." No one except an expert today reads any book written between 420 and 1100 A.D.; and if that doesn't mean a Dark Age we wonder what the word means. The writer does not even know that it was "the Father of Catholic History," Cardinal Baronius, who coined the phrase.

Even worse, from the historical angle, is the article "Democracy." It is said that "there was no room" for the idea of democracy in the Dark Age," but "Christianity with its doctrine of brotherhood and its sense of love and pity had brought into being an idea unknown to the pagan world, the idea of man's inherent dignity and importance." We resent this dumping of the sermons of priests into a modern encyclopedia, but it is even worse when the emancipation of the serfs and the granting of charters to cities are traced to that source. The purely economic causes of those developments are treated in every modern manual. What is worse, the writer conceals, or does not know, that when the democratic aspiration did at length appear in Italy the Papacy fought it truculently for two centuries. I find only one scrap of virtue in the article. American Catholics had not yet invented the myth that Jefferson got the idea of democracy from the Jesuit Suarez, so it makes no appearance here, but the writer, not anticipating it, says:

"The revolt of the colonies was not, strictly speaking, inspired by a belief in democracy though it resulted in the establishment of a republic."

How many times have I pointed that out against the Jesuits!

The article "Education" is another beautiful piece of work—from the Catholic angle. The historical part of it was written for the earlier edition by a strictly orthodox Christian schoolmaster, Welton, and was a sheer travesty of the history of education as it is now written in all manuals, yet the article in the new edition is signed "X and C.B." (Cloudsley Brereton, a British inspector of schools with not the least authority but with the virtue of faith). In point of fact it is Welton's original article a little condensed but little altered. They could not well have made it worse from the historical point of view. The abridgment has cleared away most of the few good points about Roman education, because any reference to the system of universal free schooling in Roman days clashes with the clerical slogan, which is the theme of this article, that the new religion "gave the world schools." "It was," says the writer, "into this decaying civilization that Christianity brought new life." Although only a few catechetical schools are mentioned the reader is given the impression that the new religion inspired a great growth of schools in an illiterate world. The undisputed truth is that by 350 A.D., before Christianity was established by force, there were free primary and secondary schools everywhere, and by 450 A.D. they had all perished: that in 350 the majority of the workers was literate, and by 450—and for centuries afterward—probably not 1 percent of them could read. Of course it is all put down to the barbarians. "Most of the public schools disappeared, and such light of learning as there was was kept burning in the monasteries and was confined to priests and monks." The monks were, as I have repeatedly shown from Christian writers from Augustine to Benedict, mostly an idle, loose, and vagrant class, and the few regular houses later established were interested only in religious education. Pope Gregory I forbade the clergy to open secular schools.

The article proceeds on these totally false lines through the whole of the Middle Ages. The work of Charlemagne, which is now acknowledged to have been paltry and to have perished at his death, is grossly misrepresented, and the fact that he was inspired in what educational zeal he had by the school-system of the anti-Papal Lombards is concealed. Not a word is said about the Lombard system. It is almost as bad in explaining why at last—six centuries after the Papacy took over the Roman rule—schools did begin to spread. There is just one line of reference to the Spanish-Arabs who inspired it by their restoration of the Roman system of free general education. Not a word is said about the fact that in Arab-Spain there were millions of books, finely written on paper and bound, while no abbey in Europe had more than a few hundred parchments. The origin of the universities is similarly misrepresented. It is all covered by this monstrous statement:

"On the whole it may be concluded that in medieval times the provision of higher instruction was adequate to the demand and that relatively to the culture of the time the mass of the people were by no means sunk in brutish ignorance."

"Brutish" is, of course, part of the trick. Read it simply as a denial that the mass of the people were totally illiterate and then ask yourself how it is that, even after all the work of the Jesuits and the Protestants, still by the middle of the 18th century between 80 and 90 percent of the people of Europe were illiterate. The writer is so reckless in clerical myths that he even says that the Age of Chivalry greatly helped:

"The education of chivalry aimed at fitting the noble youth to be a worthy knight, a just and wise master, and a prudent manager of an estate."

You might just as well pretend that Cinderella is a true account of certain events in the Middle Ages. The whole long article which is signed X is an outrage when it is presented to the 20th century. The falsehood is carried on over the Reformation period and into the supposed account of the real beginning of education of the people in the 18th century.

I should have to write another encyclopedia if I proposed to analyze the hundreds of articles in the Britannica which are, like this, just tissues of clerical false claims. It might be said that, like the religious literature in which these myths still flourish, the Encyclopedia has to cater to the religious public. That plea is in itself based upon an anachronism and on untruth. There is abundant evidence that today the majority of the reading public, whatever they think about God, do not accept the Christian religion. In Britain and France the clergy frankly acknowledge this, and it is concealed only by sophistry in America. But I am not suggesting that an Encyclopedia that professes to have been rewritten to bring it into harmony with modern life and thought ought to exclude religious writers. I say only that when they are entrusted with articles which are wholly or in part historical they they must conform to modern historical teaching. These articles, judged not by atheistic but by ordinary historical works, are tissues of untruth; and a good deal of this untruth, the part which chiefly concerns me here, has been inserted in the new edition by the Catholic "revisers" who lurk behind the signature X.

As this mark X is in the new edition added to the initials of Mark Pattison at the foot of the article "Erasmus" we look for adulterations. As, however, the original article softened the heresies of the great Dutch humanist there is not much change. Just a few little touches make him less important and nearer to orthodoxy, and passages reflecting on the foul state of the Church at the time are excised. With the subject "Evolution," on the other hand, no modern editor would dare to allow a Catholic writer to insert his fantastic views in a publication that professes to be up-to-date in science. But a place is found for reaction. The British Professor Lloyd Morgan is commissioned to write for the new edition a special article on the evolution of the mind, and it is based upon the eccentric theory of "emergent evolution" worked out by him in support of religion, which was dying when he wrote the article and is now quite dead in the scientific world. Next is added a section on ethics and evolution by Sir Arthur Thompson, a Unitarian whose peculiar twists of the facts of science to suit his mysticism have no place whatever outside religious literature.

The article "Galileo" would be examined eagerly by most critics for evidence of this clerical "reviser." But even in the 11th edition the article was written by a Catholic astronomer, Miss Agnes Clerke, and X seems to have been given the task of cutting her five pages down to two (while 16 are devoted to football), that gives him opportunities. He leaves untouched the statement that at the first condemnation Galileo was ordered to write no more on the subject and "he promised to obey"; which is seriously disputed and rests on poor evidence. Both Catholic writers refuse to insert the actual sentence of condemnation, which pledged the Roman Church to the position that it is "formal heresy" to say that the earth travels round the sun. When he comes to the second condemnation X suppressess Miss Clerke's hint that Galileo had ridiculed the Pope in his Dialogue, which was the main motive of the Pope's vindictive action, and attributes the procedure to Galileo's supposed breaking of his promise. He saves a precious line by cutting out Miss Clerke's perfectly true statement that he was detained in the palace of the Inquisition. In short, it is now a sound Catholic version of the condemnation of Galileo from first to last, and it does not warn the reader or take into account in the least the fact that since Miss Clerke wrote her article Favar has secured and published (in Italian) new and most important documents on the case, and they have made the character and conduct of the Pope more contemptible than ever.

The fine eight-page article on Gibbon by the learned Professor Bury in the earlier edition could not expect to escape. Space must be saved; though one would hardly realize this when one finds 60 pages devoted to Geometry, which no one ever learns from an encyclopedia. The reviser condenses the six and a half pages of Gibbon's life and character to one page and then sublimely adds his X to Bury's initials as the joint authors of the article. You can guess how much of Gibbon's greatness is left.

On the other hand the notice of Pope "St." Gregory I, the Pope who forbade the opening of schools and made the Papacy the richest landowner and slave-owner in Europe by persuading the rich that the end of the world was at hand and they had better pass on their property to the church, remains as fragrant as ever in the new edition. So does the account of Gregory VII (Hildebrand), the fanatic who violently imposed celibacy upon the clergy (impelling mobs to attack them and their wives), who put the crown on Papal Fascism, who used forgeries and started wars in the interest of the Church, who hired the savage Normans to fall upon the Romans (who then drove him into exile), etc. Naturally, the modern reader must not know these things.

The article "Guilds" in the 11th edition, by Dr. Gross, is the source of the monstrous Catholic claim that the Church inspired these medieval corporations of the workers. It is preserved in all its untruthfulness in the new edition. After a short and disdainful notice of various profane theories of the origin of the Guilds he says:

"No theory of origin can be satisfactory which ignores the influence of the Christian Church."

It was, as usual, the sublime and unique Christian doctrine of the brotherhood of man; yet this had been the cardinal principle of Stoicism and Epicureanism 300 years B.C. The statement is, in the mouth of an expert on the Guilds, breath-taking in its audacity. The documents preserved in the Migne (Catholic) collection show clearly that the Guilds were pagan in origin—they were most probably relics of the old Roman trade unions—and that the Church fought them truculently for 100 years after their appearance in Germany. Gross shows that he has read these documents. He says that the Guilds were suspected of political conspiracy and opposed on that ground. On the contrary they were denounced as pagan orgies (suppers, like those of the Roman unions, at which priests got drunk and behaved improperly.) X, of course, leaves this pious screed in all its purity.

Haeckel, like Gibbon, gets his distinction reduced in the grim need of curtailing the old articles: a need which looks peculiar when, a few pages later, General Smuts is invited to contribute a four-page article on his ridiculous "philosophy" (Holism), which has never been taken seriously. But it favors religion and—not to put too fine a point on it— Smuts rendered high political service to Britain. However, while space is so precious the reviser of the Encyclopedia finds it necessary to add this to the decimated article on Haeckel:

"Although Haeckel occupies no serious position in the history of philosophy there can be no doubt that he was very widely read in in his own day and that he is very typical of the school of extreme evolutionary thought."

The last three words give the writer away. It is only the Catholic writer who makes a distinction between schools of "evolutionary thought." As to his having been widely read, no scientific work since Darwin's "Origin" had anything like the circulation of Haeckel's "Riddle." It sold millions of copies in more than 20 languages. And a serious modern writer on Haeckel would have pointed out that while he despised philosophers and never claimed to be one, he remarkably anticipated modern thought in insisting that matter and energy are just two aspects of one reality. Of this fundamental doctrine of his the writer says not a word.

Even the article "Heresy" of the old edition, though certainly not written by a heretic, suffers the usual discriminating process of curtailment. The writer had said:

"As long as the Christian Church was itself persecuted by the pagan empire it advocated freedom of conscience . . . but almost immediately after Christianity was adopted as the religion of the Roman Empire the persecution of men for religious opinions began."

That of course is cut out. Then a long list of Catholic persecutions in the Middle Ages is cut out and replaced by this grossly misleading sentence:

"The heresies of the Middle Ages were not matters of doctrine merely (however important) but were symptoms of spiritual movements common to the people of many lands and in one way or other threatening the power of the Roman Catholic system."

An article on the subject which frankly aimed at providing facts for modern folk would have at least mentioned the death-sentence for heresy, which is obstinately kept in force in Catholic Canon Law today. Not a word about it, though on this subject of penalizing religious opinions it is the question most frequently asked today.

The article "Hospitals" gives us a choice specimen of the art of X-ing. It consist of two parts, history and modern practice. To the historical section, which it is of considerable interest to the Catholic propagandist to misrepresent, X does not append his mark, but he puts it to the section on modern practice, of which he knows nothing. Was this due to an editorial or typographical error? Listen. The old article properly gave a summary account of the ample provision for the sick in many pre-Christian civilizations, especially the Roman, and added:

"In Christian days no establishments were founded for the relief of the sick till the time of Constantine."

He might have added that even then they were few and were merely intended to keep the Christian sick away from the pagan temples of Aesculapius which were the chief Roman hospitals. All this is cut out and replaced by the totally misleading or totally false statement:

"But although hospitals cannot be claimed as a direct result of Christianity no doubt it tended to instill humanist views, and as civilization grew men and women of many races came to realize that the treatment of disease in buildings set apart exclusively for the care of the sick were in fact a necessity in urban districts."

We have several good and by no means anti-Christian histories of hospitals today. They show a fine record in India under the Buddhist

King Asoka and a creditable record for the Greek-Roman world in imperialist days. They show also that the Christian record not only in the period of confusion after the fall of Roman Empire but from 450 to the 18th century is miserable; an dthus in an encyclopedia that advertises that it is rewritten in order to ensure confidence that the reader is getting what is generally agreed upon by the experts in each department, writers are permitted to take the reader even farther away from the truth than—in articles of this kind—they were earlier in the century. A score of articles like this which are supposed to prove by historical facts the nature of the Christian social inspiration and social record are cheap and untruthful religious propaganda.

Even in the short notice of Hypatia the clerical surgeon has used his knife. Short as it was, we shall be told that it had to be curtailed (though the editor spares eight pages for Icelandic literature) but the omissions are significant. The earlier article rightly said that she was a "mathematician and philosopher," and contemporaries speak of her works on mathematics not philosophy. Yet even the word "mathematician," which does not take up *much* space does give us a better idea of the solid character of Hypatia, is cut out. The earlier writer says that she was "barbarously murdered by the *Nitrian monks* and the fanatical Christian mob," that the Caesareum to which her body was dragged was *"then a Christian church"* and that the remains of the aged scholar (as she was) were burned piecemeal. All the phrases I have italicized are carefully cut out, as is also the whole of the following passage:

"Most prominent among the actual perpetrators of the crime was Peter the Reader (cleric), but there seems little reason to doubt the complicity of Cyril (the archbishop)."

So the "correction of dates" and curtailing some articles to admit new matter" just happen to take a form which greatly reduces the guilt of the Christian Church in the foulest crime of the age; for the greatest lady in the whole Greek world at the time was stripped in the street and her flesh cut from her bones with broken pottery by monks and people directly inflamed against her by the archbishop. This is the sort of thing for which the University of Chicago now stands sponsor.

In the note on "Idealism," which is colorless, I notice that the improvers of the old Britannica have recommended a work by "G. Moyce"; a point which must rather annoy the professors since Josiah Royce is one of the most distinguished philosophers America has yet produced. More important is the great saving of space in reducing the size of the article "Illegitimacy." In face of the drivel that Catholic apologists talk about tne influence of their church on sexual conduct we have been accustomed to point out, amongst other things, that bastards are far more common in countries where the Roman and Greek churches are, or were until recent years, more powerful. In the old Britannica the article gave a wealth of statistics, particularly about Ireland, to help the student on this point. Out they have all gone—to find more space, of course, for cricket and football. "Illiteracy" is just as little seriously informing for the inquirer who wants to know whether it is true that the church is the Great Educator.

The article on "Immortality" was much too pious in the old edition of the Encyclopedia to need any "improvement." It stands, like a hundred other articles, as a monument of what respectable folk thought in Victorian days. It was out of date even in 1911. Since then the belief in immortality is almost dead in philosophy, and the teaching of psychology today emphatically excludes it. Even theologians doubt it or at least widely admit that attempts to prove it are futile. Of this state of modern thought the article gives no more idea than it does of Existentialism.

Similarly, the article "Infallibility" in the old edition was written by a Catholic and needed no "correction of dates." But it was better not to let the reader know that it was written by a Catholic, so away go his initials. The article "Infanticide" would be considered by many more important than archery and croquet and other genteel sports of our grandmothers, because it is one of the familiar claims of the apologist that while the ancient Romans were appallingly callous on the subject the new religion brought the world a new sense of the importance of even a newborn babe's life. The old edition was certainly defective in its account of practice in ancient Rome but even the little it said has been cut out. An inquirer into the subject will not get one single ray of light on Roman practice from the new article; and it is candidly signed X.

POPES AND INQUISITORS

Then we come to the long string of Popes who adopted the name "Innocent" when they donned the white robes of "the Vicar of Christ." We know little about some of them, but others are so well known, and there is so little dispute about their character, that the name is a mockery. All that the Catholic editor could do in such cases was to make a few of those neat little cuts with his scissors that at least make the record seem grayish instead of black. For instance, under "Innocent III" the old article spoke about the "horrible massacre" of the Albigensians which he ordered. The word "horrible" has been cut out; it was, no doubt, too strong an expression for the fact that only a few hundred thousand men, women, and children were savagely massacred because they would not bow to Rome. No one doubts the religious sincerity and strict personal conduct of Innocent III, but this article does not give the reader the least inkling of the perfidy, dishonesty, and cruelty into which his fanaticism led him.

It is different with Innocent VIII, an elderly *roue* who got the papacy in the fight of the factions and immensely promoted the debauchery of Rome and the Vatican. The old article said, moderately enough:

"His youth, spent at the Neapolitan court, was far from blameless, and it is far from certain that he was married to the mother of his numerous family."

As he was credited by public opinion with only 16 children the censor must have thought this excessive, so cut out the whole passage. Naturally he cut out also the later passage:

His curia was notoriously corrupt, and he himself openly practised nepotism in favoring his children, concerning whom the epitaph is quoted: "He guiltily begot six sons and as many daughters, so that Rome has the right to call him Father." Thus he gave to his undeserving son Francheschetto several towns near Rome and married him to the daughter of Larenzo de Medici (the greatest prince of Italy).

All this is cut out of the new edition of the Encyclopedia, which was to appeal to all by its accuracy. There is not the least doubt in history that the Pope had children, that his son Francheschetto was one of the vilest and most dissipated young men of Rome, and that Innocent was aware that the Papal Court was sinking deeper and deeper into corruption. The notice of the Pope in this edition is a calculated deception of the reader.

It is almost as bad with the notice of Pope Innocent X; and the deception here is the more wicked because Innocent X ruled after what Catholic apologists call the Counter-Reformation, which is supposed to have purified the papacy and the church. The notice in the old edition at least gave a hint of his character by saying:

Throughout his pontificate he was completely dominated by his sister-in-law Donna Olimpia Maidaechini (a woman of masculine

18

spirit). There is no reason to credit the scandalous reports of an illicit attachment. Nevertheless the influence of Donna Olimpia was baneful, and she made herself thoroughly detested by her inordinate ambition and rapacity.

This was a mild and inadequate expression of the notorious historical fact that for 10 years this vile woman openly sold—clerics, even bishops, queuing at the door of her palace—every ecclesiastical office in the power of the papacy; and it suppresses entirely the scandal of the Pope's "nephews." The license granted her was so enormous that folk had every reason to assume that she had been Innocent's mistress. Yet in the new edition of the Encyclopedia the main part, which I have enclosed in brackets, of the moderate passage I quoted from the older edition is cut out. An incorrect date, no doubt. Each such notice of a Pope to the middle of the 17th century is thus doctored, to protect the modern Catholic myth of a Counter-Reformation.

We come a few pages later to "Inquisition," and here you will expect that X has surpassed himself. Not a bit of it. He has changed little —because the article even in the old edition was written by a French Catholic, Alphandery. X has just touched it up a little and put his mark at the end of it. It is as scandalous a piece of deception of the public, since it is not stated and cannot now easily be verified that Alphandery was a Catholic, as for the Encyclopedia Americana to have got Japanese propagandists to write the long section in it on Japan. It opens with a show of flooring at once the critics of the Inquisition. They are supposed to say it began in the 12th century, whereas it goes back to the early church, even to Paul. This is throwing dust in the eyes of the reader. "Inquisition" does not mean persecution or prosecution for heresy but "searching out" heresy, and it was the Popes of the early 13th century who created the elaborately organized detective as well as penal force which we specifically call the Inquisition.

It next scores by remarking that the early Fathers did not favor punitive measures. How on earth could they have dreamed of them under Roman law and when they were an illicit sect themselves. It says that there was little persecution for heresy from the 6th to the 12th century, the Dark Age; which amuses us when we recall that 99 and a fraction percent of the population of Europe were illiterate and so densely ignorant that folk could not tell one doctrine from another and just attended Sunday services in Latin. Then we get the germs of the cowardly and debased modern Catholic apology: that the Church was always reluctant to persecute but the zeal of the peoples and princes of Europe forced its hand. Of course, both writers make much of the famous persecution decree of Frederic II—the great heretic who appealed to the other kings to abolish Papacy—but are careful not to mention the savage action of the papacy which dictated it or the fact that Frederic never applied the law. Torture the gentle church particularly disliked and only borrowed it from secular law: in which the church had enforced it for centuries for clerical offenses like blasphemy. They both say: "We must accept the conclusion of H. C. Lea and Vancandard that comparatively few people suffered at the stake in the medieval Inquisition." That is a total perversion of Lea's words—he refers to the first half of the Middle Ages when there was no Inquisition—and they grossly mislead the reader by coupling Vacandard's name with his. Canon Vacandard was one of the most reckless of the French apologists.

But I cannot go phrase by phrase through this Catholic rubbish. In spite of all its sophistry and suppressions it leaves the Inquisition the most scandalous quasi-judicial procedure that ever disgraced civilization, yet it is not the full truth. It is true that it does not tell the lie that American apologists now do—that the Roman Inquisition never executed men—and it does not even mention, much less challenge, the definite figure of 341,042 victims of the Spanish Inquisition which Llorente, secretary of the Inquisition, canon of the church, and Knight of the Caroline Order, compiled from its archives. Its sophistry gets it

19

so muddled in regard to this important question of the Spanish Inquisition that it first says the people regarded heresy as "a national scourge" and the Inquisition as "a powerful and indispensable agent of public protection," and then tells how the greed of the Inquisition "rapidly paralyzed commerce and industry." It does not tell how while Spain was still Catholic the fierce anger of the people destroyed the Inquisition.

This book would become another encyclopedia if I were to analyze in this way all the articles, especially on religious matters, that are in this new edition of the Britannica foisted on the reader as the common teaching of our historians, philosophers or sociologists, nor can I stop at every little specimen of the zeal of the group or phalanx of writers who mask themselves with an X. Even the article "Ionia" has suffered from their clumsy treatment. In a fine page in the last edition Dr. Hogarth summed up:

"Ionia has laid the world under its debt not only by giving birth to a long series of distinguished men of letters and science but by originating the schools of art which prepared the way for the brilliant artistic development of Athens in the 5th century."

This and the best evidence for it are cut out, but X does not put his crooked mark here. He appends it to the next section, which is on the geology of the Ionian Isles! In my own historical works I have laid great stress on the significance of Ionia and I have found my readers puzzled. They will not get much help from this mutilated article.

The historical section of the article "Italy"—a country which is described as 97.12 percent Catholics even now that Communists and Socialists dominate it—ought to have been revised, not in a Catholic sense, for it was far too lenient to the papacy, but to harmonize with the modern teaching of history. Instead of this being done X is allowed to add a gushing section on the beautiful accord of the Pope and Mussolini, the "unexampled scenes of enthusiasm" in Rome when the infamous compact was signed, and the joy of "300,000,000 Catholics" throughout the world. This in face of the notorious fact that the Fascists themselves bitterly attacked Mussolini for signing the Treaty and all that has happened since. The Chicago professors might ask Professor Salvemini what he thinks of it. The total impression given to any reader who ploughs through the history of Italy in this article from the time of Charlemagne onward is, as far as the relations of the Italians with the Popes are concerned, false; but I doubt if anybody ever does read these historical articles in encyclopedias from beginning to end.

THE JESUITS AND OTHER ROGUES

The article "Society of Jesus"—even the title has been altered from "Jesuits," a word which does not smell so sweet—ought to have been a happy hunting ground for this Catholic corrector of false dates, but from the older editions of the Britannica it had already in the 11th edition been rewritten by a Jesuit. There are, however, or used to be, Jesuits and Jesuits, and the Father Taunton who initials the article assured me that in private he went far, but one did not look for that in his professional work. His article, endorsed and relieved of any leaning to candor, is still just one of those religious tracts that the Encyclopedia offers the reader instead of seriously informing and neutral articles on controverted points. It is a travesty of the real history of the Society, a touching fairy-tale, mostly based upon what the Jesuit *professes* to be. Taunton, however, did let himself go to this extent:

"Two startling and undisputed facts meet the student who pursues the history of the Society. The first is the *universal* suspicion and hostility it has incurred—not merely from the Protestants whose

20

avowèd foe it has been, nor yet from the enemies of all clericalism and dogma but from *every Catholic state and nation in the world. Its chief enemies have been those of the household of the Roman Catholic faith.*"

For this original article gives abundant evidence. The clause I outline disappears in the sacred cause of abridgment and Father Taunton's too candid words become:

"The most remarkable fact in the Society's history is the suspicion and hostility it has incurred within the household of the Roman Catholic faith."

Much of this, he explains, is due to the superior virtues of the Jesuits and the dishonesty of their critics. He even ventures to include the austere and most virtuous Pascal in a group of critics who are described as "not scrupulous in their quotations." He cuts out the serious criticism of Jesuit education (in the old article) in order to protect the fiction, which modern Jesuits have spread, that they were great educators.

But the most deliberate perversion of the truth is seen in the account of what happened in the 18th century. It is a commonplace of history how the Catholic kings of France, Spain, and Portugal, stung by revelations of the greed, hypocrisy, and intrigues of the Jesuits, suppressed the Society in their dominions and appealed to the Pope to suppress it altogether, which he did in 1775. We might allow that in the new edition it was necessary to abridge the account of the crimes of the Jesuits on which the monarch and the Popes acted but these clerical champions of accuracy in the new edition of the Encyclopedia have gone far beyond this. Taunton had said:

"The apologists of the Society allege that no motive influenced the Pope save the love of peace at any price and that he did not believe in the culpability of the Jesuits. The categorical charges made in the document (the Pope's bull) rebut this plea."

Taunton gave enough of the Pope's words—I give a fuller account in my large "Candid History of the Jesuits" (which is, of course, not mentioned in the bibliography)—to prove this. It is all cut out, and the reader is just given the modern thumping lie of the Jesuits that the Pope expressed no opinion on the charges against them. And lest any reader or critic should be able to say that that is just the opinion of a Catholic writer, Taunton's initials have been suppressed and in this case X has not given the mark of the crook. I should like to ask the professors of the University of Chicago what they think of that.

The articles "Jesus" and "Jews" I do not propose to desecrate by analysis. They are orthodox and venerable with age. They tell the reader what all theologians but a few rebels thought half a century or more ago. Whether it is for that sort of thing that you consult a modern encyclopedia. . . . Well, please yourself. It is the same with the notice of Joan of Arc. In the old encyclopedia my friend Professor Shotwell, of Columbia, had a fair article on Joan. It was not quite up to date, but it was mildly critical. Now that Joan is turned into a saint, as part of the political deal of the Vatican and the French government, and in spite of the dire need to abridge the old edition, Shotwell's sober one and a half page notice is replaced by a three and a half page sermon by a French Catholic. Not a word about modern military opinion of her—whether she had any ability at all or was just a superstitious tonic in a jaded military world—and not a word about the new research of Miss Murray and others into the real nature of witchcraft and their conclusion that Joan was probably a member of the witch cult.

Then come the "John" Popes and prodigious feats of juggling. They had to be brought down to the customary level of grossly untruthful treatment of saints, martyrs, popes, and other sacred things in this "modern" work of reference. Of the character of most of the

Johns we know nothing but three or four of them were so notoriously vicious and otherwise devoid of interest that their portraints had to be touched up considerably. John X was decidedly one of them. Even the old article, admitting discreetly that he "attracted the attention" of a leading lady of the Roman nobility, allowed that "she got him elected Pope" in direct opposition to a decree of council (which X cuts out). But old and new editions introduce John XI as "son of Marozia and reputed son of (Pope Sergius III." This is covering up the most infamous period of the depravity of the Papacy (or any other religious authority in the world) not with a veil but with painted boards. The period was what the Father of Catholic History, Cardinal Baronius, following the few clerical writers of the period, calls "The Rule of the Whores"; and I am not here giving a vulgar rendering of the Latin. The period stinks amazingly even in Cardinal Baronius. The two chief whores who ruled the Papacy for 30 or 40 years were Theodora and her daughter Marozia (as fierce and lustful a cat as you will meet even in the history of the Middle Ages). Two Popes at least were lovers of these women and one was—not reputed to be but certainly was—the bastard of Marozia and Pope Sergius and was put on the papal throne by Marozia's orders.

Another son of Marozia's ruled Rome and the papacy for 20 years after the period that is strictly called "The Rule of the Whores" and he put his own son, John XII, on the papal throne. There may have been a few Popes as licentious as this young man was—I would not be quite sure of it—but certainly not one worse. He, says the contemporary Bishop Liutprand, turned the papal palace into "a brothel" and an inn. He seduced his father's mistress and his own sisters and raped pilgrims, he castrated the single cardinal who criticized him. . . . There was nothing he did not do during the 10 years of his pontificate, yet the the feeble reference to his scandolous private life in the 11th edition is cut out in the fourteenth, leaving him one of the Holy Fathers.

It is useless to go into every detail and is enough to say that in the case of the next scandalous John (XXIII) the work of the reviser is as foul as ever. He lived and ruled at the height of the Italian Renaissance (1410-15), and he was a monster of crime in comparison with the notorious Alexander VI. Neither the writer in the 11th edition (a French Catholic) nor the one in the 14th (anonymous) tells the undisputed fact that he was notorious for vice and corruption before he became Pope. In fact neither hints at irregularities before he was condemned by the Council of Constance. The older writer then candidly acknowledged that the Council (300 prelates) endorsed 54 charges against him and that three cardinals he paid to undertake his defense refused to do so. "Enough charges," he said, "of immorality, tyranny, ambition and simony were found proved to justify the severest judgment." As a matter of fact the indictment, which may be read in any Latin History of the Councils, was a complete inventory of crimes and sins. One sentence includes "murder, sacrilege, adultery, rape, spoliation and theft." And this precious "rectifier" of errors in the new edition cuts out the whole of this. He just states that the Pope was suspended but the sentence was irregular in canon law!

Passing on our way to the Leos we note a point here and there that need not detain us. "Jubilee year" is described as an institution of piety and not a word said about the greed and corruption of the Pope who established it and why. Julius II has had the character-sketch in the old edition. though written by a Catholic, touched up and trimmed until the reader, who may have read something in regular history about the Pope's children, his heavy drinking and swearing, and his unscrupulousness, will be surprised to find how great and virtuous a Pope he was. The greatest nobles of Rome at the time assure us that he was a sodomist. "Juvenile Offenders" is a title that ought to meet many searching and varied queries in our time. It completely fails. Not a word about religion. Not a single statistic. Then we come to the article "Knighthood and Chivalry," to which we were referred in the short note "Chivalry."

I have made considerable research on this point in medieval history and have pointed out repeatedly that the belief that there was an Age of Chivalry (about 1100 to 1400) is one of the crudest and emptiest of all the historical myths with which Catholic writers adorn their Middle Ages. No expert on the period fails to say the opposite. But in the case of this article I gather that the learned writer of it in the 11th edition, Dr. Coulton, who died in 1947, would not tolerate any monkey tricks with his work. He was not a master of the literature of the subject but he does say:

"Such historical evidence as we possess, when carefully scrutinized,, is enough to dispel the illusion that there was any period of the Middle Ages in which the unselfish championship of God and the Ladies was anything but a rare exception."

Dr. Coulton has paid too narrow an attention to the fairl-tale itself. On the broad question of the character of the princes, lords, knights, and ladies of the period, particularly in regard to sex, cruelty, dishonesty, and injustice, we have mounds of evidence, and it consistently shows that this was one of the least chivalrous and most immoral periods in history.

In the long list of the Leo Popes I need notice only the important article on Leo X, the man who opposed Luther. Here, however, X had not much to do. The article in the 11th edition was by Carlton Hayes, the Catholic professor at Columbia. It falsely said that modern research has given us a "fairer and more honest opinion of Leo X." He was "dignified": the Pope who enjoyed nothing more than grossly indecent comedies, largely written by his favorite cardinal, in the sacred palace and banquets at which gluttony was a joke and the most vulgar adventurers were richly rewarded. He "fasted"—at the doctor's orders, for his body was gross. With a show of liberality it admits that he was "worldly," "devoid of moral earnestness or deep religious feeling," "treacherous and deceptive" (which is explained away as the common policy of princes at the time). No, X did not find many "dates" to correct in this Catholic sophistication, but the man who wants truth in his encyclopedia will. Not the least idea is given of the monstrous corruption of the papal court under Leo: not a hint that it was so commonly believed in Rome that he was a sodomist that both his friends and authorized Biographer Bishop Giovio and the great contemporary historian Guiccardini notice it and, contrary to the statement of the Catholic historian Pastor, seem to believe it.

The article "Libraries" is the next on which X employs his subtle art. I have explained, I think, that X is not one encyclopedic Catholic writer who does all this marvellous work. The explanation given of the X in the first volume of the 14th edition is that it is "the initial used for anonymous writers"; just as the lady whose sins are not to be disclosed in the court is called by the police Mlle X. In all earlier encyclopedias anonymous writers, who do the great body of the hackwork of the encyclopedia, did not need any monogram. But, of course, this was a special arrangement with the Catholic body. It assumes that Committees of Catholics on both sides of the Atlantic were appointed to scrutinize all articles bearing upon Catholic myths and to cut out and modify, no matter on what authority it rested, any statement that the Catholic clergy do not like. Whether any other sort of anonymous critics were allowed to do similar work and wear the mask I do not know. I have not noticed an X anywhere except where truth has been slain or mutilated by a Catholic sword.

You may wonder why an innocent article on Libraries should excite the suspicions of the Catholic Knights Errant, but the *history* of libraries, like the history of literature or education generally, is even more dangerous from the Catholic viewpoint than an amorous story or picture. It tells how the Greeks and Romans had splendid libraries (and literature and schools); how during the Christian Middle Ages libraries (and schools and books of interest) were few and paltry to the

12th century; how in the meantime the Arabs and Persians again had magnificent libraries (and schools and literature) and in the course of two or three centuries succeeded in stimulating sluggish Christian countries to have a few decent libraries. This is real history and of deep sociological significance. But it is the kind of history Catholics hate as they hate science. So the historical part of the article is mercilessly but selectively cut.

A point, for instance, on which an inquirer is still apt to consult an encyclopedia is as to the fate of the greatest library of the ancient world, that of Alexandria. Said the article in the 1911 edition:

"In 389 or 391 an edict of Theodosius ordered the destruction of the Serapeum, and the books were pillaged by the Christians."

This is cut out, and we have to be content with a vague admission that the stupid story that "the Library survived to be destroyed by the Arabs can hardly be supported." The older writer said that the transfer of imperial powers from Rome to Constantinople was "a serious blow to literature." This truth also is cut out. He said that "during the Middle Ages knowledge was no longer pursued for its own value, but became subsidiary to religious and theological teaching." Monstrous. Out it goes.

Loisy, the great French scholar, had a couple of pages in the 11th edition. He was then still a Catholic. He is cut to a paragraph in the 14th edition. The fame of his scholarship had grown but he had openly quit the Church. When you see 20 pages devoted to logic, in which few folk take any interest today, you wonder whether the need of abridgement was really so drastic, but the pruning shears (and the signature X) appear again in the article "Lollards," who were deadly enemies of the church. It is the same with the Lombards. Instead of the short account of their great importance in the restoration of civilization in Europe being expanded, as modern interest requires, it is cut down, as the interest of the papacy demands.

"Lourdes" would seem to give X a great opportunity but the old article had only a few lines on the shrine of Lourdes. They are neatly strengthened. The older writer generously noted that it was "believed by the Roman Catholic world" that the Virgin revealed herself here. This becomes stronger. Lourdes has become famous since the visions of Bernadette Soubirons and their authentication by a commission of inquiry appointed by the bishop of Tarbes. As if no serious person doubted them. But you are referred to Catholic literature for details of the epic story of the growth and the miracles: a tissue of fabrications.

The article "Martyrs" was in the old edition an edifying Christian sermonette, and it remains. Here, in a modern and candid encyclopedia, we should have had a useful account of the mass of historical work that has been done on the marytrs, even by Catholic scholars like the Jesuit Delehaye and Professor Ehrhard, in the last 50 years. More ancient martyrs have been martyred with the axe, of historical truth than the early Christians manufactured in 200 years.

In the article "Materialism" you know what to expect. In this and most other encyclopedias Romanists write on Catholic matters, Methodists on Methodists matters and so on, but, of course, on such subjects as Agnosticism, Atheism, Materialism, Naturalism, etc., we must entrust the work to ignorant and bigoted critics. So we still read how "naive materialism" is due to "the natural difficulty which persons who have had no philosophical training experience in observing and appreciating the importance of the immaterial facts of consciousness." Some reverend gentleman has been drawing upon his sermons for copy. Not a single word about the evidence provided by Professor Leuba and others that, on their own profession, more than 70 percent of the scientific men of America are "naive materialists." With a fatuousness that makes us groan the clerical reviser adds to the short article:

"Largely through the influence of Bergson, Alexander, and Lloyd Morgan contemporary science is turning away from materialism and reaching toward the recognition of other than mechanical factors in the phenomena, even the physical phenomena, of Nature."

The encyclopedia might just as well say that under the influence of Gandhi, the Grand Lama, and the Mufti of Jerusalem, military men are now turning away from thoughts of war.

X comes on the scene again in the article on the Medici. Any truthful account of this famous Florentine family must show us the greatest paradox—if you care to call it paradox—of the Middle Ages; a wonderful art, superficial refinement, and pursuit of culture covering an abyss of corruption. The older writer was honest enough to tell a little of the background, and X generally cuts it out. The great Lorenzo is disinfected, and he strikes out such passages as this, referring to Cosmo III:

> "Cosmo's hypocritical zeal for religion compelled his subjects to multiply services and processions that greatly infringed upon their working hours. He wasted enormous sums in pensioning converts— even those from other countries—and in giving rich endowments to sanctuaries."

Lorenzo's 20 lines of vices are "abridged" into two, and so on.

"Medicine" ought, like "Libraries," "Hospitals" and a score of other articles, to show in its historical part the appalling blank in the civilized record. It did this to some extent in the earlier edition, so the account of Greek-Roman and Arab-Persian progress is abridged so that the blank from 500 to 1500 is not so painful to the eye.

"Mithraism" might seem an innocent and remote subject but the modern inquirer will want to know whether or no it is true that it made more progress than Christianity in the Roman world and whether it had a superior morality. The fine article by Professor Grant Showerman in the 11th edition fairly answered these questions. He said that by the middle of the 3rd century "it looked like becoming the *universal* religion" (which is cut out). He said that it appealed to the Romans by its strongly democratic note and its high ethic. Here his account is cut to pieces, and we now learn that it made progress by boasting of an esoteric wisdom and compromising with paganism. The substance of Showerman's article is kept but his initials are deleted. Perhaps he demanded that. Of course, nothing is said about the material borrowings of Christianity from Mithraism or how Christianity destroyed its rival by violence.

It appears that X (or one of him) is also an expert on Mohammed. He has reduced an authoritative 12-page article to three pages and perhaps some will think that he has shorn the prophet's glory. Moses on the other hand passes into the new edition as "one of the greatest figures in history." You may have heard that even theologians and liberal Jews are wondering how much historical knowledge we have of such a person, "Beyond question," says this more accurate new edition, "Moses must be regarded as the founder alike of Israel's nationality and of Israel's religion." These X's are great at settling disputed points.

The article, "Monasticism," is a grand opportunity for telling a large amount of picturesque truth. But, alas, even the editor of the 11th edition had the quaint idea that it ought to be written by a monk. The result is that X did not find a word to alter. We have the old article in all its fragrance—and mendacity. It tells us as much about the new history of the monastic bodies in Europe as a history of Hitlerism by a Fascist would tell of events in Europe. Whether or no an encyclopedia is a book in which you expect the truth, the whole truth, and nothing but the truth. . . . There are probably simple folk who do.

"Mozart" does not sound of theological interest, but since his Requiem or "mass for the dead" is said to be "one of the finest of religious compositions" and is a prime favorite in the Catholic ritual it is important to the church that the public should not learn that he was an apostle and an anti-clerical Freemason who, in the familiar phraseology of the cleric, died and was buried like a dog. The article in the old edition did not tell the whole truth about this, but its misleading of the public was not strong enough for the reviser so it is made a little more misleading. It is well known in what circumstances Mozart began to compose his Requiem. A stranger approached him and offered to pay him to write it, and, as Mozart was ailing, the story runs that he nervously saw in the offer a warning of his death. If he did so at any time he must have soon learned that (as it proved) it was a rich amateur (Count Walsegg) who was really hiring his genius, but the "reviser" of the article has actually changed the text from "Mozart worked at it unremittingly, hoping to make it his greatest work" to "Mozart put his greatest music into it and *became more and more convinced that he was writing it for his own death.*" After this you would expect a lovely death in the arms of his holy mother the church, but the clerical reviser cuts out in the new edition what the expert writer of the article said. It was:

"His funeral was a disgrace to the court, the public, society itself . . . his body was buried in a pauper's grave."

But the initials of the writer, Sid D. T. Tovey, are kept at the foot of his mutilated article. This story of a mysterious visitor who gave Mozart the idea that he was being supernaturally warned of his approaching death has recently inspired an eloquent article in the pious *Reader's Digest*. Naturally readers who turn for verification of it to the great Encyclopedia will be fully encouraged. The fact is, as the "corrector" probably knew well, Mozart refused to send for a priest when he became dangerously ill and when his wife secretly sent for one the man refused to attend so notorious a heretic. It might be instructive to the inquirer into religious inspiration in art to know that one of the most beautiful pieces of church music was composed by a man who emphatically rejected Christianity, but it would be inconsistent with so much that *is* said in the Britannica, so the fact is suppressed.

Nietzsche you would almost expect to find banished altogether from so pious an encyclopedia, but we have here one of the little mysteries of its compilation. In spite of the grim need for abridgment the one-column article in the 11th edition has been replaced by a two-page appreciation of the great skeptic by his devout follower, Dr. A. Levy. One might quarrel with it here and there but let us not be meticulous.

HOW HISTORY IS RE-WRITTEN

There must have been a good deal of maneuvering in the subterranean vaults in which the new edition of the Britannica was being forged when the time came for doing an article on the papacy. In the 11th edition the lengthy treatment of the subject was entrusted to a number of well-known Catholic writers who were understood to be what were then called "liberal Catholics." The first section, covering the early centuries and the Dark Age (to 1100), was written by Mgr. Duchesne and the next by Professor Luchaire, both said in private clerical circles (to which I once belonged) to be modernists. Duchesne was an archtrimmer, and he writes the first 1,000 years of the history of the papacy in such fashion that X finds nothing to correct. I do not know to what extent there are folk who fancy that by reading such an article they learn the historical truth, but the fact is that this long article on the papacy is a travesty of history and a sheer Catholic tract; and any subeditor ought to have known what to expect. It is utterly impossible for any Catholic writer to tell facts, much less the whole of the facts, on such subjects. How could he, for instance, tell that few historians outside the church admit that there is any serious evidence that Peter was ever in Rome? Duchesne placidly observes that it is "now but little disputed," because a few American historians who play up to Rome take an indulgent view of the so-called evidence. I have proved from the most solid Christian document of the time that the Roman Christians of the 1st century did not believe it.

So the narrative continues on the usual and most untruthful Catholic lines. All the other churches looked up to the Roman and did not question the universal authority of its bishop; which is the direct opposite of the truth, for I have shown in detail that every assertion of Roman authority over the other churches to the 6th century (when the other churches had either disappeared or formed the separate Greek Church) was indignantly, often contumeliously, spurned. There is, of course, not the slightest hint of the demoralization of the church from about 150 onward. It is a body of virtuous folk braving its persecutors. And its immense enrichment after the conversion of Constantine is explained audaciously by saying that the pagan emperors had deprived the church of its wealth and Constantine just restored it! Naturally there is not a word about the dozen persecuting decrees, even with a death-sentence, which the bishops got from the Christian emperors and so crushed every religious rival.

This fairy-tale, which it is disgusting to find in a serious encyclopedia, is sustained throughout the entire 30-page article, but I have not space here to go much into detail. There was no Dark Age for the church, though the "barbarian invasions," the usual scapegoat, are admitted to have caused some irregularities. There is not the least recognition of the need to explain why the worst degradation of the papacy, from 890 to 1050 began four centuries after the invasions and deepened for 100 years. The attainment of the Temporal Power is explained without a word about the Donation of Constantine, which Catholic historians admit to have been a forgery, and the development of the monstrous pretensions of the Popes to power is explained by an argument as ingenious as it is false. Innocent III was "compelled"—I have shown from his own letters that he deliberately and fraudulently engineered it—to sanction, though he tried to check, the persecution of the Albigensians. Then the corruption of Europe by the Renaissance "infected" the good church to some extent, but there is no proof, for instance, of the fearful charges against John XXIII. No; they were merely examined and endorsed by a Council of 29 cardinals, 33 archbishops, 150 bishops, 134 abbots, and 100 doctors of law and divinity. The second two-century period of deep papal degradation is passed over with the admission that there was one pope, Alexander VI, of abandoned morals.

X then takes up the story and you may bet that it does not lose in piety. This is how he writes history. At the French Revolution "the Pope fought against the Terror when the worship of reason was proclaimed." There, of course, never was a "worship of reason" in France, and the Feast of Reason and Liberty in Notre Dame was not official, and it was after the official proclamation of *the Worship of the Supreme Being* that the Terror followed. So on to 1929. This is, as I said, a blatant Catholic tract from beginning to end, and it closes with the usual list of popes all of whom to the year 530—including such rogues as Victor, Callistus, and Damasus—are described as "Saints." Some of them are fictitious, the majority of quite unknown character, and half the remainder poor specimens.

Catholics might well boast of their service to their church in getting permission to correct a few dates and other trifling errors in the earlier Britannica. Their converts, if educated at all, are generally of the type who would look for truth in an encyclopedia. Perhaps one ought not to complain if the editor of an encyclopedia invites a Christian Scientist to tell the aims and belief of Christian Science, Moslem to tell the tenents of Islam, and so on, but to allow Catholic propagandists not merely to explain what the Church's doctrines are but to write 30 pages of historical mendacity and misrepresentation because. . . . Well, you may guess for yourself what the agreement between the contracting parties was. Where the Chicago professors come in I don't know.

Presently we come to the article "Pasteur," and of course that famous scientist must be claimed as a Catholic, though I have proved a

27

score of times that he quit the church early in his career, publicly avowed his Agnostic creed, and died without any recognition of the church. There was a fine article on him in the earlier edition by Sir Henry Roscoe, which concluded:

"Rich in years and honors, but simple-minded and as affectionate as a child, this great benefactor to his species passed quietly away."

In the new edition this becomes:

"Rich in years and in honors, this simple and devout Catholic, this great human benefactor. . . ."

And there is no X to warn the reader that an anointed hand has altered the article. That happens in hundreds of cases.

Psychical research was still considered by many in the first decade of this century to be at least not a waste of time, so three pages were devoted to it in the 11th edition. In the third decade of the century few took any serious notice of its futilities, yet. in spite of the tremendous need for abridgment, the three-page article is replaced by a five-page article by an enthusiast for the nonsense. The article "Psychology" is, of course, entirely useless to any inquirer who wants to know, as most thoughtful folk do want to know, what the modern science makes of the old idea of mind. You gather that the mind is still as solidly established as the Pope. With great boldness (it seems to think) the new article alters the definition of psychology from the science of the mind to "the study of the mind or of mental phenomena." At the time (1929) there was hardly a manual published in America that did not define it as "the science of behavior" and reject the reality of mind. But the new article does not give you the least idea of the revolution. Two reactionary professors just grind out five pages of the old academic verbiage. It is like a barrel-organ in Broadway.

"Preaching" is a short article which few folk will ever consult, but there is here a point of high social interest. When good people read about the way in which the church kept men in the ways of virtue during the Middle Ages—one of the most vicious of historical periods— they imagine devout priests preaching the gospel to them every Sunday. It is all a myth, of course. The faithful just spent half an hour to an hour in church on Sunday morning while the priest raced through the liturgy of the mass, in Latin, which quite commonly he did not understand himself. The friars of the later Middle Ages created quite a sensation when they began to preach sermons. But does our E. B. tells the reader this? Look up the orthodox short article.

"Rationalism" is a companion article to "Agnosticism," "Naturalism," and a score of other articles. It is just a moldly piece of academic verbiage. It tells you how once there were bold thinkers like Hume and Kant who thought that truth was to be learned by the use of reason not intuition. but of the mental attitude which 99 men out of 100 call Rationalism today, of its great growth in the 19th century and the reasons for this, it does not say a word.

The Reformation is still a subject of high popular interest in countries where the population is divided into Catholics and Protestants, and we may regret that the fine 20-page article by Professor Coulton in the 11th edition is reduced to nine pages in the 14th. We do not forget the imperious need for abridgment though when we notice that 36 pages are spared for Pottery and Porcelain, that Psychical Research gets more room than ever. and so on, we are a little puzzled. And, as usual, the abridgment happens to cut out bits that Catholics do not like. In both editions the article has the initials of Professor Coulton. a learned liberal Protestant expert on the Middle Ages who wrote with discretion and reserve; that is to say, he said far less about the share of the appalling general corruption of the Church in causing the Reformation and far more* about political conditions than a quite candid historian would today. However. as Coulton was still alive and active in 1929 I imagine that he saved his article from the Catholic chopping block.

The article "Relics" also is written by so lenient a Protestant writer that it is little altered. The reader will not get from it the faintest idea of the appalling fraud in the manufacture of relics in the early and the medieval church, the gross traffic in bogus articles, and the exploitation of the people.

On the important subject of the Renaissance one may congratulate the editors on having carried into the 14th edition the splendid article by J. A. Symonds. They could hardly venture to do otherwise, for Symonds is incomparably the highest authority and best writer on the subject in the English language. But the cloven hoof appears here and there. We get the ridiculous contention of certain second-rate American professors that it is misleading to speak of "the Renaissance," meaning that Christian Europe had been asleep until the 13th century. There had been a "Carolingian Renaissance" in the 9th century, an "Ottonian Renaissance" in the 10th. and so on. Unforunately it was precisely after these "rebirths" that Europe, especially Italy, sank to the lowest depth. To call these claims "new historical research" is bunk. They are symptoms of the demoralizing growth of Catholic influence in America. What is really new is the research into the causes of the rebirth of Europe after about 1050, which has shown the great debt of the Christian world to the Arabs and Jews. Preserved Smith seems here to do the X-ing and he not only is too pious to tell the truth about the influence of the Albigensians and the wicked Spanish Arabs but he appends to Symonds' fine article a rather incoherent page comparing the Renaisance and the Reformation as "emancipations."

But the Catholics expand gloriously when we come next to the article "The Roman Catholic Church." In the older edition the introductory part was by the old-fashioned historian Alison Phillips, and he is now replaced by a short—well, say fragment of a sermon—by no less a person than Cardinal Bourne (assuring us in effect, that as the Roman Church alone was founded by Christ we need not pay any attention to other churches) and a technical account of the structure of the church by a theologian. But the 10 pages of history, now written by a priest, that follow are just the same undisguised propaganda with a sublime indifference to the facts as non-Catholic historians tell them. You have here, in fact, the clotted cream of Catholic controversial literature served up in an encycloepdia that promises you an objective statement of modern culture and scholarship. There are few statements of fact in it that have not been torn to shreds years ago.

You have the old story of the Christian body surviving 10 persecutions by the pagans. We thought that it had been agreed by this time that there were only two general persecutions in 250 years, but this new encyclopedia accounts says that there were 10 or actually there was one long struggle. How even Catholic scholars have shown that only a hundred or two of the many thousands of martyrs claimed have survived scrutiny, how the bishops of the time describe the enormous body of the faithful abjuring the faith—Catholics claim 10,000,000 Christians in the time of Diocletian and can't prove 100 martyrs—and so on, is, of course, not mentioned. The growth of the church's power, spiritual and temporal, is described in the usual Catholic manner. Even in the Dark Age— a phrase that does not soil this article. of course—the Roman Church was "the most vigorous influence for civilization in Western Europe"— on its own theory it took six or seven centuries to civilize it—and if it seems to turn its spiritul power into political repeatedly it was compelled to do this because the secular princes wanted to "control the souls of men." I should be inclined to call that the high-water mark of Catholic rhetoric. We are given to understand that during these centuries (500 to 1300), apart from a little disorder caused by the barbarian invaders, the church kept the world (and its clergy, monks, and nuns) virtuous— that is one of the tallest myths in history—but "the pagan Renaissance" and "the general decadence of morals" which this caused unhappily did penetrate the armor of the church's virtue a little. It seems that even many of the Popes themselves were too affected by the general materialism." A grave work of reference offers us that as a summary of the historical fact that, to say nothing of the barbarism of the Dork Age and the license of the 12th and 13th centuries, the papacy itself was so low in tone from 1300 to 1670 that the few popes who made a serious effort to reform the church—and that in regard to sex almost alone—reigned, collectively, only about 20 years out of the 350 and the general level of conduct in Europe was infamous. And it is equally false to say that the church purged itself by a Counter-Reformation which began before and independently of its Protestant critics. The Reformation began in 1517, and the Vatican and Rome were, as the contemporary Cardinal Sachetti describes, appallingly corrupt to 1670. This is public instruction in history up to date, and now under the aegis of the University of Chicago.

One of the arch-sophists of the American regiment of propagandists, Mgr. Peter Guilday, is permitted to tell the situation of the church in the world today. It is enough to repeat what he says about America. He says that in 1920 there were 22,233,254 Catholics in America so there were probably about 25,000,000 (the Catholic Directory claimed only 20,000,000) in 1928. The same church authorities give these enormously conflicting figures, yet notice how definite they are to the last unit. Naturally he does not explain that, unlike any other church, the Catholic Church includes in its figures even the millions who have quit it. On such positive inquiries as we have it seems that there can hardly be much more than 15,000,000 real Catholics in America; but it would not do to let Washington know that.

After this I need not comment on the article "Rome," meaning the city of Rome. The sketch of its history during the Dark Age and the later Middle Ages is on a line with what I have just described. Compared with the great work of Gregoravius, the world-authority on the city, this account is like a Theosophist's sketch of the life of Mme. Blavatsky. "Russia" must have tempted the ghostly censors, but the editor of the Encyclopedia got Duranty to do it, and we miss the clerical touch. "Skepticism" is another subject on which, you would think, a Catholic would like to write but the article was already so innocuous and misleading that it was left in all the glory of its Victorian verbiage. The poor man who has to depend upon encyclopedias for his information will gather that Skepticism was, like Rationalism, a malady of the philosophical world in the last century but that it has died out.

Under "Schools" there was in the 11th edition a fine 12-page history of schools in Europe from Greek-Roman days onward. After what we saw about he articles "Education" and "Libraries" you will be prepared for a burnt offering. The whole essay, with its excellent account of the Roman system of free schools for all, and discreet insinuation of the blank illiteracy and schoollessness of the Dark Age, and some account of the Arab-Persian achievement, goes by the board. Certainly it was important to provide large new space for modern school systems, but an informed and honest pedagogist could have told the historic truth and introduced the results of recent research into the Spanish Arab-Schools in a page or so. But it would have been deadly to the claim that Christianity "gave the world schools" or that the Roman Church cared the toss of a cent about the education of the children of the workers until secular states started our modern systems.

In passing we note how neatly the Encyclopedia does a little whitewashing of the church in the Dark Age in its article "Silvester II." We do not question that he was "the most accomplished scholar of his age"—in Christendom, the writer ought to have added. He is not to be mentioned in the same breath as Avicenna (Ibn Sind), the great Persian scholar of the same age, and could not hold a candle to scores, if not hundreds, of other contemporary Persian and Arab writers. But what the article and Catholic writers generally carefully conceal is that he got his learning from the Arabs—his chief biographer proves

30

that he actually studied in Cordova (and had a gay time there)—and that he was forced by the German Emperor upon the reluctant and half-barbarous Romans, and they probably poisoned him off in four years. He was a great collector of books (manuscripts), but, says this article ingenuously "it is noteworthy that he never writes for a copy of one of the Christian Fathers." Read his life by the expert and you will smile.

"Slavery" is an article upon which a critic would joyously pounce if he did not know anything about the Irish professor Ingram, who wrote the long and fairly good articles in the 11th edition. Ingram was a Positivist and he let the church off lightly, as Positivists always do; and at the same time let the public down heavily. But even Ingram's dissertation was a little too strong, so X was let loose upon it, and he adds his mark to Ingram's initials as joint author. You know why the subject is important from the clerical angle. The myth that Christianity "broke the fetters of the slave" is so strongly established, though it has not an atom of foundation, that even the late H. G. Wells included it as a historical fact in the first edition—he promptly cut it out when I told him how wrong he was—of his "Outline of History." Neither St. Paul nor any Christian Father nor any Pope or great Christian leader, and certainly no Church Council, condemned slavery until modern times when the wicked "world" was busy extinguishing it. Even the article in the "Encyclopedia of Religion and Ethics" makes this clear. It still existed in Europe, though economic conditions had greatly restricted it, when, under the blessing of the Spanish Church, it expanded again into the horrible chapter of African slavery. The proper treatment of Ingram's article would have been to let the reader understand this more clearly, to take into account the large amount of scholarly work which has in recent years greatly modified the old idea of slavery in Rome in the first three centuries of the present era, and to explain how economic causes changed slavery to serfdom and then, in most of Europe, emancipated the serfs. Instead of this X has been permitted to do a little of his usual tampering with the truth.

"Solomon" has a page and a half of the old credulous glorification, in spite of all the progress of biblical science. If this and similar articles which were solemnly read by our grandmothers but are now confined to the seminaries of the more backward churches, such as the Catholic, had been cut down to so many explanatory short paragraphs, the editor might have found room for a couple of useful pages on Social Progress, though the subject deserves as much space as football or cricket: and at least a couple (instead of the scanty and outdated treatment of the subject under "Psychology") of pages summarizing the results of the important new science of Social Psychology.

The historical section of the article "Spain" ought to have been almost entirely rewritten. It was written in the days when historians had not quite recovered from the Catholic legend that the Arabs had taken over the beautiful Christian country in the 8th century and held an eccentric rule over it until the valiant Spaniards overthrew them and made the country glorious and virtuous once more. For 100 years we have known the truth, and since this article was written liberal Spanish professors—Ballesteros, Ribera, Cordera, etc.—working on the Arabic manuscripts which have been hidden in Catholic libraries for centuries so that the orthodox myth should not be exposed, have shown the real grandeur of the Arab (as opposed to the later Moorish) civilization. The churches of the Christian monarchs themselves and the remarkable sexual looseness of the Spanish clergy and people in all ages have been established, the appalling ruin of the country after 100 years of Castilian rule has become a platitude of history, and even the Cambridge History tells the awful story of the Bourbon dynasty in the 19th century and, in conjunction with the church, its savage war on liberalism. It is impossible to understand modern Spain unless you know these things. The Encyclopedia does not tell them. It completely misleads the innocent reader and supplies as "authority" an untruthful religious propagandist.

The article on Spiritualism was entrusted to Sir Oliver Lodge, a man who had betrayed his childlike credulity and unfitness for such a task in his "Raymond" and other works. There are six pages on "Spirits" and they will doubtless have a use for experts in distillation (who ought to know all about it), but on the subject of "Spirit," which is one of the most confused words in the modern vocabulary, there is not even a paragraph. Writers, preachers, and politicians talk every day about "spiritual realities," and we may surely assume that a large number out of their tens of millions of readers and hearers would like to know precisely what they mean. From a wide experience I may say that most of them do not know themselves. One American professor gives us seven different definitions of the word Spirit. Yet editors who spare many pages for whelks or wall-papers give no assistance here. Naturally the British (High Tory) journalist, Garvin, who was the original editor of the 14th edition, knew no more about these things than Henry Ford or Herbert Hoover did. What the editor whose name appears on the latest printing of it, Walter Just, knows I can't say, as his name is not in "Who's Who in America." But there must have been a regiment of sectional editors, and this is their idea of giving the general public clear ideas and authenticated facts to enable them to form sound opinions.

The article "Stoicism" is not much less misleading. There is so much extant literature of Stoicism—Epictetus, Seneca, Marcus Aurelius, etc.— that it was in modern times impossible to misrepresent it as the philosophy of Epicurus is misrepresented (the early Christians having conveniently burned the whole of his 200 books). So pious folk swung to the opposite extreme. It was a religion founded by an austere puritan named Zeno and was too high and impractical for the people. The article in the Britannica runs on these lines. The author puts out of all proportion the small and temporary religious wing of the movement and misrepresents the character of Zeno, who, his Greek biographer tells us, used to go with a youth or a young woman occasionally to show that he had no prejudices of that sort. He fails entirely to make clear that the central doctrine of the Stoics, the Brotherhood of Man, was a practical social maxim borrowed from the gay-living Lydians, and that it was a blend of this with the same central doctrine of Epicurus that worked as an inspiring social influence in the Greek Roman world for five centuries; and that of the so-called Stoic emperors only Marcus Aurelius, who let down the Empire, was a Stoic.

MORE WHITEWASH FOR THE MIDDLE AGES

An article on Surgery is scarcely the place in which you would look for clerical trickery, and X has not ventured to couple his name with that of the distinguished expert who writes the article in the 11th edition. But his work has in the 14th edition been deprived of an essential value. I do not know many who consult such articles as anatomy, physiology, surgery, and medicine in an encyclopedia. They are too technical for the general public, while students have to seek their information in more serious works. But the historical introduction which the Britannica used to prefix to its essays on the more important branches of science and on such subjects as education, slavery, philanthropy, etc., were useful to a wide public. Reading the articles in the 14th edition, one would at first think that the editors had never heard that anybody disputed the claim that the churches created modern civilization. The truth is, of course, that the historical introductions to articles on the various elements of our civilization in the old Britannica made a mockery of the clerical claims and painfully exposed the barbarism of the Dark Age and the scientific sterility of the later Middle Ages. In those days the clerical bodies had not the economic and business organization that they now have, and they had to be content that they were allowed to write the articles on religious subjects, that articles dealing with philosophy, psychology, and ethics were entrusted to men of the old spiritual school, and that the general historical sections were carried on from the less critical days of the last century. Now even the scientific parts must be revised. Those introductions which brought out too prominently the cultural blank of ages in which the church was supreme must be abbreviated by cutting out significant details, falsified, or abolished.

In this case the excellent four-page introduction on the historical development of surgery has disappeared. It had shown that, while there was appreciable progress in the science in Greece and Alexandria, this was lost in the general barbarism after Europe became Christian.

"For the 500 years following the work of Paulus of Aegina (the last distinguished Greek surgeon) there is nothing to record but the names of a few practitioners of the court and of imitators and compilers. . . . The 14th and 15th centuries are almost without interest for surgical history."

The writer admitted, however, that the Arabs and Persians had resumed the work of the Greeks, and, though they were occasionally hampered by the religious ban on dissection, they carried the science forward once more. In point of fact this article ought here to have been strengthened, for in some respects the Arabs advanced far beyond the Greeks. But all this is as distasteful to our modern clerical corporations as statues without fig-leaves, so the whole section has been cut out. We fully recognize that a great deal more space was needed for modern sugery but there are hundreds of articles of far less importance to the modern mind that could have been relegated to the 19th-century trash-basket.

The next article that attracts the critical eye is "Syllabus," the account of a miserable blunder that the papacy committed in 1864 in condemning a long series of propositions (on liberalism, toleration, freedom of conscience, etc.) most of which are now platitudes even to the Republican or Conservative mind. If Catholic writers in America did not now pretend that their church had always accepted these principles of social morals and public life, if they did not lie about the nature of their Syllabus, no one would complain if this egregious blunder of the rustic-minded Pope Pius IX were reduced to a short paragraph, provided it was truthful. The article in the 11th edition was written by a French priest but it did give the reader some idea of the monstrosity of the condemnation. It has been abbreviated—but cutting out all details that conflict with the modern Catholic-American version of the Syllabus.

We cannot grumble because the lengthy article on the Templars by a distinguished historian of the last century, Alisen Philips, has been cut from eight pages to five, but when we see that X has added his unsavory mark to Philips' initials as joint author of the article in the 14th edition our suspicions are aroused. Few of the general public now have the dimmest idea, at least in America—in London and Paris a whole area still bears their name (the Temple)—who these Knights Templars, or Knights of the Temple of Solomon, were, but their shameful story is an important part of our moral indictment of the Church in the Middle Ages, and the Catholic apologist not only misrepresents it but quotes them as a grand example of the inspiration of his faith. This small society of monastic knights was formed in Jerusalem about the year 1120 precisely because the Crusaders who had settled in Palestine were comprehensively and appallingly corrupt; so corrupt that only eight out of the whole body of knights were willing to adopt the stricter life. Pious folk, as usual, showered wealth upon the new monks—the "brutal pious, simple-minded men," as Professor Langolis calls them—and by the end of the century they were a rich and corrupt body all over Europe. In 1309 the Pope was compelled, by his deal for the tiara with the French king, to put them on trial for corruption, and a great trial by the leading lawyers of France, four cardinals appointed by the Pope, and a number of French prelates was held at Paris.

X improves Philips' article by first distracting attention from the fact (which even Philips did not accentuate) that the trial of the Templars was one of the conditions on which the Pope got the French king to secure the papal throne for him, and then cutting out the worst charges that were made against the Templars. They were accused of not only a general practice of sodomy, which (as recent trials in Germany showed) is a normal vice of celibate religious bodies, but of *compelling* members of the Order to practice it. At initiation, it was said, each had to kiss the Grand Prior's nude rear, spit on the crucifix, and worship an effigy of the devil. Suppressing these charges certainly cheats the reader, who is given to understand that their immense wealth just led the monk-knights into familiar irregularities. The mere fact that priests brought these foul charges against one of the best known orders of monks in the beautiful 13th century, before the "pagan Renaissance" tainted Europe (as these revisers say in a previous article), and that they were proved to the satisfaction of a group of cardinals, archbishops, and great lawyers is a social phenomena. So the charges are cut out.

Under a series of horrible tortures (including torture of the genitals) most of the monk-knights, including the Grand Master and his chief assistants, admitted the charges. The tortures used are another appalling reflection on the age and its courts, so these, though well known in history, are not described in detail, but the reader is invited to regard confessions made under torture as worthless. What would you think of a body of monks and knights (of the Age of Chivalry) who, to escape torture, would confess that they practiced, and their whole body had practiced for decades, the most degrading vices, besides wholesale drunkenness and other evils, and that they had sacrificed children to the devil in their nocturnal orgies As to the impossible nature of the charges, remember that the witches, who had begun to spread over Europe, did almost the same things, except that they healthily detested sodomy and did not sacrifice children or virgins.

However, we cannot go further into the matter here. Historians have always been divided as to their guilt—mainly because they have inadequate ideas of the character of the time—but X has blurred the mild and insufficient account of the trial that Philips gave and he has—I would almost say the insolence—to say in the end that the Order of the Templars had "deepened and given a religious sanction to the idea of the chivalrous man and so opened up to a class of people who for centuries to come were to exercise influence in spheres of activity the beneficent effects of which are still recognizable in the world." The Age of Chivalry, we have seen, is a sorry myth, but to speak of the Templars as one of its ornaments. . . . It stinks. He adds that they also "checked the advance of Islam in the East and in Spain." The last check on the advance of the Moslem in the East had been over nearly a century earlier and they had made no attempt to advance in Spain for two centuries before the Order of the Templars was founded.

The articles "Theism" and "Theology" were, of course, so thoroughly sound from the clerical point of view in the 11th edition that there was no call for revision. In the article on Theism the space is mainly occupied with a long account of the old-fashioned proofs of the existence of God: Cosmological, Teleological, Ontological, Ethical and from Religious Experience. I do not know how many folk are saved from Atheism every year by studying these evidences in an encyclopedia, but I think it is a pity the Catholic censor was not let loose here. Not that he would have criticized the arguments. They are venerable relics of his own Thomas Aquinas. But as Fulton Sheen says in his "Religion Without God," "the Catholic Church practically stands alone today in insisting on the power of reason to prove God." A blatant exaggeration, like most of what Sheen says, but wouldn't it have been proper to warn readers that, as William James said of these arguments, for educated folk "they do but gather dust in our libraries." See the different article "Theism" in the Encyclopedia of Religion and Ethics.

But X comes upon the scene once more "Thirty Years War," the account of the long and bloody struggle of Protestantism for existence in the 17th century. In face of the elementary fact that the Catholic powers, led by the fanatical Spanish Emperor, were entirely on one side —except France, which Cardinal Richelieu who defied the Papacy, kept out—and the Protestant powers on the other, it would be ludicrous to deny this most devastating struggle in Europe between the 5th and the 20th century the title of a religious war, but Catholic writers try to magnify such political elements as it had and to conceal from the reader the debasement of character which it caused and the way in which it set back the progress of civilization in Europe more than 100 years. Here X uses his pen and his blue pencil freely and then gaily adds his mark—it used to be the mark of folk who could not write their names —to the initials of the original writer, Atkinson, as joint author.

Certainly it was necessary and desirable to cut down the dreary eight-page chronicle of battles and movements of armies, but the main improvement should have been to make clearer from recent literature the share of the Vatican and the Jesuits in bringing about the war and the attitude of Richelieu toward the papacy. X, of course, does the opposite.

Atkinson says in the original article, for instance:

"The war arose in Bohemia, where the magnate, *roused by the systematic evasion of the guarantees to Protestants,* refused to elect the Archduke Ferdinand to the vacant throne."

This is a mild expression of the fact that the Jesuits had got their pupil Ferdinand to break his oath to the Protestants, but X changes it to:

"The war arose in Bohemia, where the Protestant magnates refused to elect Ferdinand of Austria to the vacant throne."

The Jesuits, who haunted the Catholic camps, are never mentioned, the Vatican rarely. Richelieu's defiance of the Pope is concealed. The terrific degradation of character—one Catholic army of 34,000 men had 127,000 women camp-followers—and the destruction, especially of the old Bohemian civilization—its population of 3,000,000 was reduced to 780,000—are concealed from the reader, while he gets five pages of miserable battles and outrages (like the burning of Magdeberg with its people in their homes) that may have served as an inspiration to Hitler.

No candid article on the Thirty Years War would be complete today without an account of the behavior of Pope Urban VIII, who in the article on him is simply charged with "nepotism." It was a nepotism, the Catholic princes then said and many modern Catholic historians admit, that lost the Catholic powers the war. For decades the Popes had stored a vast quantity of gold in the Castle of Saint Angello in anticipation of this war on the Protestants. The Vatican and the Jesuits were as determined to wipe out European Protestantism in blood as some are now eager to extinguish Communism. In the closing years of the war the Catholic generals called for this fund and said that with it they coul dsecure victory. But the Pope had distributed most of it, and ultimately distributed all of it, amongst his miserable relatives. The famous historian L von Rank estimates the sum at, in modern values, more than $500,000,000. Recent Catholic histories of the Popes—Hayward's and Seppelt and Loffler's—admit the facts. Naturally X does not say a word about them, and Atkinson apparently did not know them.

On Toleration there is no article, so we are spared the contortions of the Catholic writer who proves, as easily as we prove the wickedness of theft, that in a Catholic country no tolerance must be extended to other sects, but in all countries where Catholics are in the minority they are entitled to full toleration, if not privileges. You may have read the bland words of Mgr. Ryan, the great moral philosopher of the American Catholic Church, on the subject: "Error has not the same rights as truth." Whether the X bunch did not think it advisable to give their views on toleration or the editors did not think it advisable to publish them is one of the little secrets of this conspiracy. Certainly those members of the public who are interested in such questions would find an up-to-date article on religious freedom, which after all is fairly widely discussed in our time, more useful than a thousand articles or notices which linger in the Britannica from Victorian days.

The article on Torquemada, the famous Spanish Inquisitor, in the 11th edition was written by the Jesuit Father Taunton, and although he was, as I have earlier noted, more liberal than a good Jesuit ought to be, Catholics had little fault to find with the article. But his judgment on the character of the fanatic, which is the only point of interest about him to us moderns, was repugnant to the Catholic revisers of the 14th edition. Taunton had said:

"The name of Torquemada stands for all that is intolerant and narrow, despotic and cruel. He was no real statesman or minister of the Gospel but a blind fanatic who failed to see that faith, which is a gift of God, cannot be imposed on any conscience by force."

This is the general verdict of historians, but the new Britannica must not give the general verdict of historians when it is distasteful to Catholics. So the paragraph is cut out. Again, while Father Taunton—once more in agreement with our historians—says that Torquemada burned 10,000 victims of the Inquisition in 18 years the reviser inserts "but modern research reduces the list of those burned to 2,000." As no signature is subjoined while Taunton's initials are suppressed, the reader is given to understand that this correction of Llorente's figures is given on the authority of the Britannica. As a matter of fact, what the writer means is that one or two Catholic priests like Father Gams have been juggling with the figures so as to bring down enormously Llorente's figure of the total victims of the Spanish Inquisition. Their work is ridiculous. Llorente was not only for years in high clerical dignity and esteem in Spain, but, as its secretary, he had the archives of the Inquisition and copied from them. But this is one of the new tricks of Catholic writers. Saying that "recent research" or "recent authorities" have corrected some statement about their church they give a few names of priests, knowing that the reader never heard of them and and suppressing the "Rev." or "Father." A priest can become an expert on a section of history as well as any man but he will never tell the whole truth about it and he will strain or twist the facts at any time in the interest of his church.

The next article I select for examination reminds us that the Catholic group of twisters that operates under the banner X—the straight, not the crooked, cross—are not the only pious folk who have been allowed or summoned to revise the Britannica from a peculiar angle. It is the article "Torture." The long and generally sound article in the 11th edition had to be abridged in the 14th edition and Professor G. W. Keeton, now Professor of International Law at London University, was entrusted with the work; doubtless to the annoyance of the X group.

For any attempt to whitewash the Middle Ages is up against the notorious fact that cruelty and torture, both judicial and extra- judicial, prescribed in codes of law or practiced by individual rulers (of states or cities) or owners of serfs, knights, and even 'ladies,' were more common and more horrible, especially in what is called the brighter (later) part of the Middle Ages (to the 18th century) than in any other period of civilized history except, perhaps, in China and in certain ages in

Persia. This was not made plain enough even in the older article by Professor Williams. He almost confined himself to a study of the prescription of torture in codes of law. But he did give the reader such warnings as:

"Thus far the law. In practice all the ingenuity of cruelty was exercised to find out new modes of torment."

Elsewhere he warns that where torture was not prescribed in the law it "certainly existed in fact." Keeton, who uses Williams' article with few additions, emits these warnings and just deals with law. The title of the article is "Torture" not "Torture in Law Codes," and it is the terrific, horrible daily use of torture that rebukes the church.

The truth is that Keeton is a pious member of the Church of England, and he is no more willing than X to admit that Christianity kept the world at a low level of civilization. He makes the general remark that the nations of Europe borrowed the practice from ancient Rome—as if a man could excuse his crimes by pleading that he simply copied them from a civilization which he professed to regard as pagan and vicious—and he darkens the case against the Romans. Even when he reproduced Williams' list of Roman opponents of torture he has to put St. Augustine on a common level with Cicero, Seneca, and Ulpian. But Williams had given Augustine's words. He said that evidence given under torture was unreliable but he "regarded it as excused by its necessity." Keeton omits this and falsely says that Augustine "condemned it." When he goes on to name modern critics—he cannot name a single one between the 5th century and the 16th—he does not seem to know that six out of the eight he names were notorious Skeptics and the other two were regarded as Skeptics. He can find only one Christian who condemned the bestiality and *he* (Augustine) did *not* condemn it. He does worse than this. The old article began its section on the Church. It said:

"As far as it could the Church adopted Roman Law. The Church generally secured the almost entire immunity of the clergy, at any rate of the higher ranks, from torture by civil tribunals but where laymen were concerned all persons were equal. In many instances Councils of the Church pronounced against it; *e.g.*, in a synod at Rome in 384."

The learned professor of international law—when you want accuracy, of course, you have to get a professor—turns this into:

"The Church, although adopting a good deal of Roman law, was at first definitely opposed to torture."

All that he gives in support of this is the "synod at Rome in 384." And there was no such synod: see Bishop Hefele's "History of the Councils." What there was in 384 was a small synod at Bordeaux, on the very fringe of the Empire, and even there only one bishop censored the torture of heretics. In France, said the old article, "torture does not seem to have existed *as a recognized practice* before the 13th century." Keeton cuts out the italicized words. As a matter of fact chronicles of the Dark Age (Glaber in the 10th century, etc.) tell of an appalling volume of torture (castration, boiling oil, etc.) in France centuries earlier. In the case of England Keeton contrives to give the reader the idea that torture was much less, but any full English history shows that in the 12th century, for instance, England groaned with daily torture as foul as the Chinese. The whole article is scandalously misleading.

"Trent, the Council of" is an article in regard to which a conscientious Catholic reviser must take great care that the full truth is not told. The article in the 11th edition is by a liberal Protestant ecclesiastical historian and although it did not contain errors and was not calculated to inflame Catholics, it did not bring out the points which any truthful dissertation on the subject must emphasize today. Too many of these professors imagine that it is their business in such articles to give a dry and accurate string of dates and movements, ignoring the lessons for our own time. The Catholic apologist wants the modern reader to regard the Council of Trent as the chief item in the Counter-Reformation or the Church's own work of purifying itself of abuses quite independently of the pressure of the Reformers. This, though now a commonplace of American Catholic literature, is a monstrous distortion of the facts, and as far as Trent is concerned, the article, even if it gave only the main facts, shows it.

The Council was forced upon Rome by the German Emperor who threatened to bring his army to Italy, and was meant primarily to cleanse the whole church of the comprehensive corruption which the German prelates freely described in early sittings of the Council. For years Rome refused to summon it and then decided to make the Council formulate a standard of doctrine by which it could judge and eventually (in the Thirty Years War) wipe out the heresy. Several abortive attempts were made to open the Council, as the Emperor saw (he said) that the Pope (brother of the girl-mistress of Pope Alexander VI) was bent only on "the suppression of heresy." In the middle of the struggle this Pope, Paul III, died and, as if to show that the papal court was determined to protect its gay life, the cardinals elected an even worse man, Julius III; a man whose gluttony, heavy drinking, gambling, and delight in obscene comedies are admitted by the Catholic historian Pastor, while the Romans of the time seriously charged him with sodomy (while he was Pope) with a disreputable Italian boy whom he made a cardinal. But the Germans intimidated him, and he had to summon the Council. Mirbt's article in the 11th edition mildly (concealing the Pope's low character) said:

"Pope Julius II, former Legate Del Monte, *could not elude the necessity of convening* the Council again, though personally he took no greater interest in the scheme than his predecessor in office, and caused it to resume its labors."

Even this temperate expression of the truth is too much for our Catholic corrector of dates and other trifles. He alters it to:

Pope Julius III, the former Legate Del Monte, caused the Council to resume its labors."

With a few touches of that sort he turns Mirbt's half-truth into a travesty of history. It was not until Julius died that the Vatican got a Pope with a zeal for chastity (and a furious temper, a love of strong wine and long banquets, and a shameful nepotist). He lasted four years, and his successor was a man of the old vicious type, so that, as Pastor admits, "the evil elements immediately awakened once more into activity." This was half a century after the beginning of the Reformation and, if Catholic writers were correct, the Counter Reformation. But I must here be brief. The Council closed in 1563, and the Papacy was still in a degraded condition a century later. Yet the revised article on the Council of Trent makes it appear a zealous and successful effort of virtuous Popes to purify the church.

The article "Tribonian" may seem negligible from our present angle but it has an interest. Amongst the feats of Christianity in the early part of the Dark Age we invariably find the Justinian Code, or the code of law compiled, it is said, by the Emperor Justinian. As Justinian, who married a common prostitute, thought about little above the level of the games of the Hippodrome, this seems incongruous, but it is well known to historians and jurists that the code was compiled by his great lawyer Tribonian. The interest is that, as Dean Milman shows, Tribonian was not a Christian but the last of the great pagan jurists. In the 11th edition this was at least hinted. In the 14th the whole discussion of his creed and half the appreciation of his work disappear.

"Ultramontanism" also is doctored in the new edition. Mirbt had given a perfectly fair account of this extreme version of the claims of the papacy. Until the last century—in fact, until 1870—there was far more resentment of the papal claims in the national branches of the church than there is today, and they used the word ultramontane as a term rather of contempt for the extreme propapalists. The article has been considerably modified to conceal from the reader this earlier attitude of defiance of the Pope on the part of large numbers of Catholics.

"Utilitarianism" is, since the social theory of morality is hardly noticed in the reactionary article "Ethics," the section in which the reader ought to be informed on the conception of morals in which is the alternative to the Christian conception. And it is today a matter of primary importance that this information should be provided in an encyclopedia. When 70 percent of American scientists, sociologists, philosophers and historians privately admit and allow the fact to be published that they have no belief in God and therefore no allegiance to the Christian or theistic code of morals—when there is plain evidence that this is the atttiude of 70 percent of the better-educated public and that at least half the general public come under no Christian influence (in advanced countries where statistics are not so loose at least 60 to 70 percent)—an account of the purely humanist or social conception of moral law, as it is now elaborated in most manuals of the science of ethics, is far more important than the lives of hundreds of half-mythical saints or monarchs and accounts of a thousand objects or ideas in which few are now interested. It is the more urgent because, owing to the clerical domination in our time of the press, the radio, and education, our people are confronted daily with the dogmatic assertion that the Christian conception of morality is the only effective version and that when it is rejected the social order disintegrates.

From every point of view a thorough and practical statement of the social theory, supported by ample statistics showing the relation of crime and other disasters to the degree of religious instruction in a state, is one of the essential requirements of a modern popular education. Instead, if our sociologists and pedagogists were as courageous as they are skilful, they would insist upon the incorporation of that code of conduct in the school-lessons, whatever other ideas of behavior religious folk liked to have their children taught in sectarian schools. The dual standard of conduct today is not one law for the male and one for the woman but the confusion in ideas of the code of all conduct: yet the new edition of the Britannica sins worse than the old, which had a good article by Sturt on the evolution of what used to be called the Utilitarian theory in philosophy. This old word is now misleading and too academic. The article is retained on the same grounds as "Skepticism," "Naturalism," etc., written by clerics or philosophers of the last century. The encyclopedia is careful to adjust itself to every change in industry or art but it pleases the reactionary by ignoring as negligible the corresponding changes in social and political matters, which are far more important.

On the other hand it can find plenty of space for a new, legnthy, and gorgeously flattering article on the Vatican by a Roman prelate; an article which talks, for instance, about the tomb of St. Peter as smoothly as if no one questioned its genuineness, whereas it would be difficult to name a non-Catholic historian who admits it. Certainly one expects in a modern encyclopedia an account of both the magnificent Vatican architecture and the structure and functions of the complex Roman court (curia) of today. But even this is not truthful when it comes from a Catholic pen. There ought to be a section, on some such lines as George Seldes's work, at least on the volume and sources of the Vatican's income and modern policy.

As to the article on the Vatican Council (1870) which follows, it is a temperate objective account by Mirbt adroitly touched up and made misleading by X. It is important to know two things about this Council. Its chief work was that for the first time in the history of the Roman Church it declared the pope personally infallible, by no means in all his utterances (encyclicals, etc.) but when he claims to use his gifts

39

of infallible guidance. The important point to the modern mind is that there was a massive opposition of the bishops present to accepting such a dogma, and it was only by the use of bribery and intrigue and after long days of heated quarrelling—I have heard the description from men who were present—that the Vatican won its way. The second point is that the papal triumph was rather like the painted scenery of a theater. The papal theologians had before them the long list of all the doctrinal blunders that Popes have made since the 4th century and had to frame the definition in such terms as to exclude these blunders. The world has seethed with problems as it never did before, and simple-minded Catholics have crowed over Protestants that *they* have "a living infallible guide"; but he has never opened his infallible lips. He has just blundered on with fallible and reactionary encyclicals as Popes have done since the French Revolution. Naturally all suspicion of these things has been eliminated from the article.

Modern-minded inquirers might have expected articles on the Virgin Birth and Vitalism, but a candid discussion of the former would have exposed the gulf that is opening on the subject in the theological world itself, and an article on the latter would either have been too boldly untruthful or it would have betrayed how materialistic science has become. In an earlier comment I noted that these "revisers" tell the reader in one article that under the influence of Bergson, Lloyd Morgan, Sir Arthur Thompson, and similar men science has become less materialistic. These men were Vitalists, claiming that there is something more than matter and physical and chemical energies in living things. They were a clique of scientific men or philosophers who allowed religious views to color their science and had no influence on others. Vitalism is dead. Thousands of thoughtful Americans would like to know why, while physicists like Millikan and Compton are always ready to stand up for the faith, hardly one distinguished biologist can be persuaded to support them. A truthful article on Vitalism would have given the answer.

The article on Voltaire in the 11th edition was a five-page essay by Professor Saintsbury, a paramount and critical authority, yet, although no one can pretend that recent research has added to or modified our knowledge, the Vatican detectives were let loose upon it. Some writer who suppresses his name used Saintsbury's material and falsified his conclusions. He suppresses such details as the fact that Voltaire built a church for the pious folk among whom he lived. He inserts these things in Saintsbury's estimate of Voltaire's character:

"He was inordinately vain and totally unscrupulous in gaining money and in attacking an enemy, or in protecting himself when he was threatened with danger."

Saintsbury, who was no blind admirer of Voltaire had said:

"His characteristic is for the most part an almost superhuman cleverness."

Now we read:

"His great fault was an inveterate superficiality."

It is a mean article, preserving the general appearance of the impartiality of a great literary critic and inserting little touches here and there to spoil it. As Noyes's book is the only addition to the bibliography one wonders. . . . But it is one of the few articles of that length in the Encyclopedia that is not signed. Saintsbury had been less generous than the famous liberal and learned cleric Dr. Jowett, who says in one of his letters: "Voltaire has done more good than all the Fathers of the Church put together." It was not in the interest of accuracy that the anonymous reviser used his pen.

There is no need here to search every short article that touches religion in the Encyclopedia for "correction of dates and other trifles." Running cursorily over the remaining volume I am chiefly interested in the omissions. I look for some notice of recent psychological research on what is still called "Will" and I do not find a word except on the legal document known as a Will or Testament. We hear folk still all round us talking about strong will and weak will, good will and bad will, the will to believe, and so on, but the very word is dropping out of manuals of psychology, and specific research in American psychological laboratories has reported that there is no such thing as will in man's make-up. We could chose a hundred short articles to omit in order to give a little space for these important changes in psychology. But doubtless it would have encouraged the Materialists, who are damned from the preface of the work onward.

But let me say one good word for the Encyclopedia before I come to the end of my list. Only a week ago I read a new novel, by a Catholic writer, who takes himself seriously. It was based upon the author's firm—in fact impudent and vituperative as far as the rest of us are concerned—belief that witches exist today and worship a devil who is as real as Senator Vandenburg or Mr. Molotov. In fact, the pompous idiot clearly believes that beautiful but naughty young ladies still fly through the air by night on brooms! I think he makes his virtuous heroine estimate the speed at about 30 miles an hour. Here, I reflected, is a man who takes his facts and views about religion from our purified Encyclopedia, and I turned to the article "Witchcraft."

To my astonishment I found that the article in the 14th edition is by Margaret Murray, whose learned and admirable work on witchcraft ought to have made a final sweep of these medieval ideas. Of course, there were witches, millions of them in every century after the 14th, of all ages, from babies dedicated by their mothers and beautiful young girls to the aged (who seem to have been the less numerous), of both sexes, of every social rank and often of high clerical rank. Of course, they believed that they were worshipping a real devil (the Spirit) and were sexually promiscuous in their nocturnal meetings, which ended in orgies. There were no broomsticks, werewolves, or magical powers. The local organizer was a secret man who at the meetings generally dressed in a goat's skin (and often horns) and had probably a stone or bone or wooden phallus to meet the demands on him. Of course, there was a lot of crookedness. But the "witches" were genuine folk, who, finding themselves in a world in which hundreds of thousands of "holy persons" grew fat by preaching a religion of chastity and self-torture while in practice they smiled upon and shared a general license, preferred a frank cult of the Spirit that blesses human nature and its impulses. Miss Murray was not granted space enough to explain this fully, or hers would have been one of the most interesting articles in the new encyclopedia. But we like the unexpected breath of realism as far as it goes.

Unfortunately, we soon find that this does not mean that the editors were converted or had a jet of adrenal energy in the 23rd hour. In the article "Woman" we again detect the hand of the reactionary. We recognize that the great development of woman's activities in modern times required a large amount of new space, and that since the editors were determined for some reason to keep to something like the proportions of the old encyclopedia a good deal of abridgment was required. But, as happens in scores of cases of these articles the abridgment has meant the suppression of a vast amount of material which the Catholic clergy did not like. No sensible man will regard that as a mere coincidence.

Since the reconstruction of the Britannica in 1911 two things happened in this connection. One was the development of new feminist activities and organizations for which, we recognize, new space had to be found. The other was a development of a political sense which led to a vast amount of anti-clericalism amongst the women. Since the beginning of the last century a small minority of women have pointed out that the historical record of woman's position and refusal of her rights reflected bitterly on the Christian churches, especially the Roman, and their claim that "Christianity was always the great friend of woman" (and of the child, the sick, the slave, the worker, etc.). This claim was, as usual, a flagrant defiance of the facts. In the great old civilizations, Egypt and Babylonia, woman's right to equality was recognized. In the Greek-Roman civilization, which began with profound injustice to her, she had fairly won her rights before the end came. But the establishment of Christianity thrust her back into the category of inferiority and she suffered 14 centuries of gross injustice; and the champions of her rights from the time of the French Revolution onward, both in America and Europe, were for the far greater part Skeptics, and the clergy opposed them until their cause showed promise of victory in the present century.

The article "Woman" in the 11th edition had an historical introduction which, though by no means feminist, gave a considerable knowledge of these facts. It has entirely disappeared from the 14th edition instead of being strengthened from the large new literature that has appeared since 1914. Exigencies of space, yes. We know it. But as in the case of dozens of others articles the clergy wanted these historical sketches buried.

We might say the same about the workers, but even in the old edition the editors had not dared to give a sketch of or a summary of the facts about the position of the workers in the Greek-Roman world in imperial days and then in the Christian world from the 5th century to the 19th. That would smack of radicalism. A large new literature has since appeared; and certainly here no one will plead that there is a lack of public interest. But in this connection we understand the feeling of the editors. Any candid account today of the privileged position of the workers in imperial Rome and their awful position during the 14 Christian centuries that followed would bring a shower of familiar missiles (Reds, Bolsheviks, Atheistic Communists, Crypto-Communists, etc.). We grant it: But the other side must grant what obviously follows. They have to suppress a large and pertinent body of truth in works of public instruction at the bidding of vested interests, clerical and other, and leave the reactionaries free to disseminate untruth.

It is the same with the final article I select, "World-War II." The time will come when truths that are still whispered in military and political circles will be broadcast, and this article will be charged with suppressing or obscuring facts which are of great importance for a sound judgment on the conduct of the war, particularly in regard to the criminal neglect to make such preparation for it as might have so far intimidated the Nazis, Fascists, and Japanese that they would not have made the venture. But what concerns me here is the complete and severe suppression of any reference to the share of religion and the churches in inspiring and supporting the war or confirming the scandalous period of sloth that preceded it.

Three things are today certain. The Vatican and its national branches are red to the shoulders with the blood that was shed. From the outbreak of Franco's rebellion—the curtain-raiser of the war—and the trouble in Czecho-Slovakia to the year when Russia turned the tide against the Germans and an Allied victory seemed at least probable the Roman Church, in its own interest, acted in the closest co-operation with the thugs. One can quote even Catholic writers (Teeling, etc.) for that. The second is, that the Japanese religion, Shinto and Buddhism alike, were similarly, in fact openly, working with the blood-drunk Japanese leaders. This was emphasized at a World Congress of Religions in Chicago several years before the war broke out. Thirdly, the Protestant churches in America enfeebled the warning against Japan, in the interest of their missions, the Lutheran Church in Germany bowed servilely to the Nazis except when Hitler interfered with its doctrines, and the British churches were equally guilty in the pre-war period. This attitude of the organized religions was of vital use to the aggressors. But we couldn't tell that, the editors of the Encyclopedia will protest.

And that is just one of the grounds of these criticisms. The Encyclopedia Britannica does not tell the reader facts and truths if the clergy do not like them, and that covers a considerable territory in regard to history, science, and contemporary life. The 14th edition not only does not tell them but suppresses them if earlier editions told them, and even allows untruths to be inserted.

POISONING THE WELLS

By a curious coincidence—so odd that the reader may be a little skeptical but I give my word for it—on the very day on which I write this page I get a letter from an American correspondent who treasures his Encyclopedia Britannica and avails himself of a recent offer of the publishers to send free replies to any questions it may inspire. I gather that he gets these replies from the University of Chicago. It is always a graceless and painful thing to distrust any man's faith in academic human nature but when my friend reads this little book I wonder if he will retain his confidence in all its robustness.

The professors will doubtless reply at once that I seem to expect en encyclopedia which is written for the service of the general public to include Rationalist opinions or at least to allow its writers to make positive statements on controversial matters, which is a sin against the ideal of educational publications. To the first of these complaints I would reply that Rationalism is now the attitude of a much larger proportion of the reading public than Christian belief is, yet in a thousand signed articles or short notices in the Britannica Christian writers are permitted to express their peculiar opinions and convictions freely, it would hardly be an outrage to expect the editors to allow Rationalists to provide the accounts of Rationalism, Skepticism, Naturalism, Atheism, Agnosticism and scores of similar articles which bear upon their position. But that they have not done so but have invariably hired hostile theologians to mangle these subjects is the smallest and least important criticism that I have here expressed. Of course. I do not expect them to act differently. Rationalism is unorganized and has no influence on the circulation of large and expensive works that are mainly destined for reference libraries. But is there any harm in drawing the attention of the public who use the books to that fact?

Well at least, they will say, McCabe expects to find the views which Rationalists take on controverted subjects embodied in the work. Again I do nothing of the kind. I might plead once more that as the majority of the serious reading public are no longer Christians they have the same right to have the critical view of a particular issue brought to the notice of Christian readers as these have to have *their* views forced upon the Rationalist. Has the capital invested in the Encyclopedia Britannica been provided by the Sacred Congregation for Propagating the Faith, the Catholic Welfare body, the Knights of Columbus—somehow my mind asks a question or two at this point—the British Catholic Truth Society or Westminster /Federation. the Episcopal Church, the Methodists, or the Baptists? The earlier editions of the Britannica were published in days when the immense majority of those who consulted the book were Christians. It chooses to act today as if there had been no change. We, of course, know why. The cost of producing such a work and the profit on it have mainly to be secured from public or college or other institutional libraries, and these are to an enormous extent, especially in America, subject to a clerical censorship. I am too faithful a realist to make the welkin ring with my complaints because the publishers recognized this situation. Or am I churlish because I draw the attention of the public to the fact that this situation has an influence on the contents of the book

I would not even embark upon these considerations only that I know from 50 years experience that what I *do* say will be ignored or misrepresented and the public will be distracted from my real criticisms by triumphant refutations, rich in irony and rhetoric, of something that I did *not* say.

The candid reader hardly needs me to re-state the chief grounds of my analysis of the work. The main idea is stated plainly in the introductory pages. I had occasion a few years ago to take up the matter. I have myself little need to look for my information, except perhaps a date occasionally, in encyclopedias, and when I do I generally collate the British, American, French, German, Italian, and Spanish, all of which are equally available to me. But I had, as I said, assured a correspondent that he would find proof of the castrated singers of Roman churches even in the Britannica, and this led to my discovery that the 14th edition differed materially in article after article from the 11th. (The 12th, 13th, 15th, and 16th are not "editions" in the proper sense but reprints). And pursuing this inquiry I discovered that the editors of the 14th edition had come to some remarkable secret arrangement with the Catholic Church. I say "secret" because, as I showed, the Westminster Catholic Federation with which the compact was made, though American priests assisted in the work, was compelled to make a public and humiliating disavowal of what it had claimed. Otherwise, the public would never have heard that there had been any arrangement.

For the first time I have now had the leisure to make an extensive though not complete comparison of the two editions, and the reader has seen that the second statement of the Westminster Federation—that they had simply altered dates and technical points about their church—is false. Any person familiar with these matters will assume that the bargain really was that if they were permitted to scratch out everything in the 11th edition that was, in the familiar phrase, "offensive to Catholics," they would recommend even nuns to admit it into their libraries (possibly with the anatomical and some other plates cut out) and would not oppose it in the public libraries. I doubt if it was part of the bargain that they could insert new matter that was "agreeable to Catholics," except such things as the cardinal's sermonette on the sin of birth control and the Roman prelate's publicity of the Vatican (and the genuine tomb of St. Peter).

However, as we have seen, pious zeal cannot be content with mere excisions. Give a priest an inch and he will take an ell of a lot. He does not learn casuistry for nothing. Under cover of the need of abbreviation he has deleted whole paragraphs, even columns of facts which were offensive to him because they flatly contradicted what he said or wrote, and then, possibly fearing that he had cut out too much, he inserted sentences or paragraphs which "put the Catholic point of view." He has taken phrases or paragraphs of the original writers of the articles and, while rtaining their initials, he has repeatedly turned them inside out or has said that "recent research" (the gymnastic of some other Catholic apologist) has corrected his statements.

And I say that for an encyclopedia to allow this and not candidly explain it to the public but even try to prevent the Catholics disclosing it is a piece of deception. The writers who did the work had not the decency—or were they forbidden?—to give their names, as other contributors do. It is therefore possible that the plea may be urged that various groups of folk were engaged in the work of correcting errors in the 11th edition and it was thought best to lump all these little men together as Mlle. X. We are, however, intrigued by the fact that all these alterations, suppressions, and additions that I have examined *uniformly serve the interests of Catholic propaganda* and are generally characterized by the familiar chief feature of that propaganda—untruthfulness.

Possibly the plea will be made that most of these are cases of historical statements, and that the Catholic has a right to object to the inclusion of any statement upon which historians are not agreed. I have pointed out one fallacy here. When the Catholic objects that "historians" dispute a point he generally means that it is disputed by historians of his own church: the men who say that Peter was buried at Rome and Torquemada burned only 2,000 heretics, that the Dark Age was bright with culture and virtue and the Age of Chivalry and the Crusaders irradiated the entire world, that the church was just tainted a little by a wicked world at one time but it soon purified itself by a Counter-Reformation, that there was horrible butchery at the French, Russian and Spanish Revolutions, that the Christian church abolished slavery and gave the world schools, hospitals, democracy, art, and science, and a thousand other fantastic things. If encyclopedias propose to embody these self-interested antics of Catholic propagandists the public ought to know it. In this little work I let them know it. Just the sort of thing an Atheist would do, you may reflect.

In not a single one of these criticisms have I complained that a majority-view of historians or scientists or other experts has been given to the public without reserve, though it is considered proper in serious works of history or science to add that there is a dissentient majority-view. My complaint has been throughout that even the majority-view of historians has been suppressed or modified and the evidence for them cut out where the Catholic clergy do not like that particular view to reach the public because it conflicts with what they say; and that in scores of cases statements which are peculiar to Catholic writers and opposed to even the majority-opinion of experts have been allowed to be inserted as ordinary knowledge. I have given a hundred instances of this, many of them grossly fraudulent and impudent. In short, the 14th edition of the Britannica has been used for the purpose of Catholic propaganda.

I do not in the least say that it is the only work of public reference that has been so used. The new Encyclopedia Americana betrays a lamentable degree of Catholic influence, and even the more scholarly Encyclopedia of Religion and Ethics has curried favor with Catholics by entrusting a number of important articles ("Inquisition," etc.) to Catholic writers, with the usual disastrous results; while manuals of European, especially medieval, history by some American professors strain or suppress evidence scandalously to suit Catholic authorities. I have here merely given the definite evidence in one field that the Catholic Church uses its enormous wealth and voting power to poison the wells of truth and to conceal from the public the facts of history which make a mockery of the fantastic claims it advances today.

Beyond this I have given many examples of the outdated character of a monstrous amount of stuff in the Encyclopedia that ought to have been displaced (instead of sound historical sketches) to make room for new matter. That is a natural vice of an old encyclopedia; or so we should be inclined to say if new encyclopedias did not, in order to get the patronage of reactionary institutions, imitate them. Who wants in a modern encyclopedia the mass of stuff about saints and martyrs, which are to a great extent pure fiction and rarely honest, about ancient kings, queens, and statesmen about whom the sketches lie glibly or are loaded with dates and events of no use to us, about a thousand points of theology and ritual which ought to be confined to a religious encyclopedia. It is not alone in regard to the Catholic Church that our works of reference are so full of calculated untruths and outdated obsequiousness. Although, as I said, the section of the public that ever consults one of these large works—60 to 70 percent never do—is predominantly non-Christian we do not expect the full truth, especially in regard to history, in them. The domination of the economic corporations of the clergy is too complete to permit that. I have a small Rationalist Encyclopedia presently appearing in London which I wrote six or seven years ago. It will show how different the truth, gathered from the works of experts, is from the stuff one reads in encyclopedia-articles on matters affecting one's philosophy of life; though I fear it will be issued in two expensive volumes, instead of the cheap fortnightly parts (as originally intended) of my larger American publications, and my labor will be virtually wasted; for the clergy will see that public libraries do not get it. It is a lamentable situation, for from the religious field this modern manipulation of truth extends to many others. I hope this short investigation will help to open the eyes of the American public to its new mental slavery.

Of Heaven and Earth: Essays Presented at the First Sitchin Studies Day, edited by Zecharia Sitchin. ISBN 1-885395-17-5 • 164 pages • 5 1/2 x 8 1/2 • trade paper • illustrated • $14.95

God Games: What Do You Do Forever?, by Neil Freer. ISBN 1-885395-39-6 • 312 pages • 6 x 9 • trade paper • $19.95

Space Travelers and the Genesis of the Human Form: Evidence of Intelligent Contact in the Solar System, by Joan d'Arc. ISBN 1-58509-127-8 • 208 pages • 6 x 9 • trade paper • illustrated • $18.95

Humanity's Extraterrestrial Origins: ET Influences on Humankind's Biological and Cultural Evolution, by Dr. Arthur David Horn with Lynette Mallory-Horn. ISBN 3-931652-31-9 • 373 pages • 6 x 9 • trade paper • $17.00

Past Shock: The Origin of Religion and Its Impact on the Human Soul, by Jack Barranger. ISBN 1-885395-08-6 • 126 pages • 6 x 9 • trade paper • illustrated • $12.95

Flying Serpents and Dragons: The Story of Mankind's Reptilian Past, by R.A. Boulay. ISBN 1-885395-38-8 • 276 pages • 6 x 9 • trade paper • illustrated • $19.95

Triumph of the Human Spirit: The Greatest Achievements of the Human Soul and How Its Power Can Change Your Life, by Paul Tice. ISBN 1-885395-57-4 • 295 pages • 6 x 9 • trade paper • illustrated • $19.95

Mysteries Explored: The Search for Human Origins, UFOs, and Religious Beginnings, by Jack Barranger and Paul Tice. ISBN 1-58509-101-4 • 104 pages • 6 x 9 • trade paper • $12.95

Mushrooms and Mankind: The Impact of Mushrooms on Human Consciousness and Religion, by James Arthur. ISBN 1-58509-151-0 • 180 pages • 6 x 9 • trade paper • $16.95

Vril or Vital Magnetism, with an Introduction by Paul Tice. ISBN 1-58509-030-1 • 124 pages • 5 1/2 x 8 1/2 • trade paper • $12.95

The Odic Force: Letters on Od and Magnetism, by Karl von Reichenbach. ISBN 1-58509-001-8 • 192 pages • 6 x 9 • trade paper • $15.95

The New Revelation: The Coming of a New Spiritual Paradigm, by Arthur Conan Doyle. ISBN 1-58509-220-7 • 124 pages • 6 x 9 • trade paper • $12.95

The Astral World: Its Scenes, Dwellers, and Phenomena, by Swami Panchadasi. ISBN 1-58509-071-9 • 104 pages • 6 x 9 • trade paper • $11.95

Reason and Belief: The Impact of Scientific Discovery on Religious and Spiritual Faith, by Sir Oliver Lodge. ISBN 1-58509-226-6 • 180 pages • 6 x 9 • trade paper • $17.95

William Blake: A Biography, by Basil De Selincourt. ISBN 1-58509-225-8 • 384 pages • 6 x 9 • trade paper • $28.95

The Divine Pymander: And Other Writings of Hermes Trismegistus, translated by John D. Chambers. ISBN 1-58509-046-8 • 196 pages • 6 x 9 • trade paper • $16.95

Theosophy and The Secret Doctrine, by Harriet L. Henderson. Includes *H.P. Blavatsky: An Outline of Her Life,* by Herbert Whyte, ISBN 1-58509-075-1 • 132 pages • 6 x 9 • trade paper • $13.95

The Light of Egypt, Volume One: The Science of the Soul and the Stars, by Thomas H. Burgoyne. ISBN 1-58509-051-4 • 320 pages • 6 x 9 • trade paper • illustrated • $24.95

The Light of Egypt, Volume Two: The Science of the Soul and the Stars, by Thomas H. Burgoyne. ISBN 1-58509-052-2 • 224 pages • 6 x 9 • trade paper • illustrated • $17.95

The Jumping Frog and 18 Other Stories: 19 Unforgettable Mark Twain Stories, by Mark Twain. ISBN 1-58509-200-2 • 128 pages • 6 x 9 • trade paper • $12.95

The Devil's Dictionary: A Guidebook for Cynics, by Ambrose Bierce. ISBN 1-58509-016-6 • 144 pages • 6 x 9 • trade paper • $12.95

The Smoky God: Or The Voyage to the Inner World, by Willis George Emerson. ISBN 1-58509-067-0 • 184 pages • 6 x 9 • trade paper • illustrated • $15.95

A Short History of the World, by H.G. Wells. ISBN 1-58509-211-8 • 320 pages • 6 x 9 • trade paper • $24.95

The Voyages and Discoveries of the Companions of Columbus, by Washington Irving. ISBN 1-58509-500-1 • 352 pages • 6 x 9 • hard cover • $39.95

History of Baalbek, by Michel Alouf. ISBN 1-58509-063-8 • 196 pages • 5 x 8 • trade paper • illustrated • $15.95

Ancient Egyptian Masonry: The Building Craft, by Sommers Clarke and R. Engelback. ISBN 1-58509-059-X • 350 pages • 6 x 9 • trade paper • illustrated • $26.95

That Old Time Religion: The Story of Religious Foundations, by Jordan Maxwell and Paul Tice. ISBN 1-58509-100-6 • 220 pages • 6 x 9 • trade paper • $19.95

Jumpin' Jehovah: Exposing the Atrocities of the Old Testament God, by Paul Tice. ISBN 1-58509-102-2 • 104 pages • 6 x 9 • trade paper • $12.95

The Book of Enoch: A Work of Visionary Revelation and Prophecy, Revealing Divine Secrets and Fantastic Information about Creation, Salvation, Heaven and Hell, translated by R. H. Charles. ISBN 1-58509-019-0 • 152 pages • 5 1/2 x 8 1/2 • trade paper • $13.95

The Book of Enoch: Translated from the Editor's Ethiopic Text and Edited with an Enlarged Introduction, Notes and Indexes, Together with a Reprint of the Greek Fragments, edited by R. H. Charles. ISBN 1-58509-080-8 • 448 pages • 6 x 9 • trade paper • $34.95

The Book of the Secrets of Enoch, translated from the Slavonic by W. R. Morfill. Edited, with Introduction and Notes by R. H. Charles. ISBN 1-58509-020-4 • 148 pages • 5 1/2 x 8 1/2 • trade paper • $13.95

Enuma Elish: The Seven Tablets of Creation, Volume One, by L. W. King. ISBN 1-58509-041-7 • 236 pages • 6 x 9 • trade paper • illustrated • $18.95

Enuma Elish: The Seven Tablets of Creation, Volume Two, by L. W. King. ISBN 1-58509-042-5 • 260 pages • 6 x 9 • trade paper • illustrated • $19.95

Enuma Elish, Volumes One and Two: The Seven Tablets of Creation, by L. W. King. Two volumes from above bound as one. ISBN 1-58509-043-3 • 496 pages • 6 x 9 • trade paper • illustrated • $38.90

The Archko Volume: Documents that Claim Proof to the Life, Death, and Resurrection of Christ, by Drs. McIntosh and Twyman. ISBN 1-58509-082-4 • 248 pages • 6 x 9 • trade paper • $20.95

The Lost Language of Symbolism: An Inquiry into the Origin of Certain Letters, Words, Names, Fairy-Tales, Folklore, and Mythologies, by Harold Bayley. ISBN 1-58509-070-0 • 384 pages • 6 x 9 • trade paper • $27.95

The Book of Jasher: A Suppressed Book that was Removed from the Bible, Referred to in Joshua and Second Samuel, translated by Albinus Alcuin (800 AD). ISBN 1-58509-081-6 • 304 pages • 6 x 9 • trade paper • $24.95

The Bible's Most Embarrassing Moments, with an Introduction by Paul Tice. ISBN 1-58509-025-5 • 172 pages • 5 x 8 • trade paper • $14.95

History of the Cross: The Pagan Origin and Idolatrous Adoption and Worship of the Image, by Henry Dana Ward. ISBN 1-58509-056-5 • 104 pages • 6 x 9 • trade paper • illustrated • $11.95

Was Jesus Influenced by Buddhism? A Comparative Study of the Lives and Thoughts of Gautama and Jesus, by Dwight Goddard. ISBN 1-58509-027-1 • 252 pages • 6 x 9 • trade paper • $19.95

History of the Christian Religion to the Year Two Hundred, by Charles B. Waite. ISBN 1-885395-15-9 • 556 pages. • 6 x 9 • hard cover • $25.00

Symbols, Sex, and the Stars, by Ernest Busenbark. ISBN 1-885395-19-1 • 396 pages • 5 1/2 x 8 1/2 • trade paper • $22.95

History of the First Council of Nice: A World's Christian Convention, A.D. 325, by Dean Dudley. ISBN 1-58509-023-9 • 132 pages • 5 1/2 x 8 1/2 • trade paper • $12.95

The World's Sixteen Crucified Saviors, by Kersey Graves. ISBN 1-58509-018-2 • 436 pages • 5 1/2 x 8 1/2 • trade paper • $29.95

Babylonian Influence on the Bible and Popular Beliefs: A Comparative Study of Genesis I.2, by A. Smythe Palmer. ISBN 1-58509-000-X • 124 pages • 6 x 9 • trade paper • $12.95

Biography of Satan: Exposing the Origins of the Devil, by Kersey Graves. ISBN 1-885395-11-6 • 168 pages • 5 1/2 x 8 1/2 • trade paper • $13.95

The Malleus Maleficarum: The Notorious Handbook Once Used to Condemn and Punish "Witches", by Heinrich Kramer and James Sprenger. ISBN 1-58509-098-0 • 332 pages • 6 x 9 • trade paper • $25.95

Crux Ansata: An Indictment of the Roman Catholic Church, by H. G. Wells. ISBN 1-58509-210-X • 160 pages • 6 x 9 • trade paper • $14.95

Emanuel Swedenborg: The Spiritual Columbus, by U.S.E. (William Spear). ISBN 1-58509-096-4 • 208 pages • 6 x 9 • trade paper • $17.95

Dragons and Dragon Lore, by Ernest Ingersoll. ISBN 1-58509-021-2 • 228 pages • 6 x 9 • trade paper • illustrated • $17.95

The Vision of God, by Nicholas of Cusa. ISBN 1-58509-004-2 • 160 pages • 5 x 8 • trade paper • $13.95

The Historical Jesus and the Mythical Christ: Separating Fact From Fiction, by Gerald Massey. ISBN 1-58509-073-5 • 244 pages • 6 x 9 • trade paper • $18.95

Gog and Magog: The Giants in Guildhall; Their Real and Legendary History, with an Account of Other Giants at Home and Abroad, by F.W. Fairholt. ISBN 1-58509-084-0 • 172 pages • 6 x 9 • trade paper • $16.95

The Origin and Evolution of Religion, by Albert Churchward. ISBN 1-58509-078-6 • 504 pages • 6 x 9 • trade paper • $39.95

The Origin of Biblical Traditions, by Albert T. Clay. ISBN 1-58509-065-4 • 220 pages • 5 1/2 x 8 1/2 • trade paper • $17.95

Aryan Sun Myths, by Sarah Elizabeth Titcomb, Introduction by Charles Morris. ISBN 1-58509-069-7 • 192 pages • 6 x 9 • trade paper • $15.95

The Social Record of Christianity, by Joseph McCabe. Includes *The Lies and Fallacies of the Encyclopedia Britannica,* ISBN 1-58509-215-0 • 204 pages • 6 x 9 • trade paper • $17.95

The History of the Christian Religion and Church During the First Three Centuries, by Dr. Augustus Neander. ISBN 1-58509-077-8 • 112 pages • 6 x 9 • trade paper • $12.95

Ancient Symbol Worship: Influence of the Phallic Idea in the Religions of Antiquity, by Hodder M. Westropp and C. Staniland Wake. ISBN 1-58509-048-4 • 120 pages • 6 x 9 • trade paper • illustrated • $12.95

The Gnosis: Or Ancient Wisdom in the Christian Scriptures, by William Kingsland. ISBN 1-58509-047-6 • 232 pages • 6 x 9 • trade paper • $18.95

The Evolution of the Idea of God: An Inquiry into the Origin of Religions, by Grant Allen. ISBN 1-58509-074-3 • 160 pages • 6 x 9 • trade paper • $14.95

Sun Lore of All Ages: A Survey of Solar Mythology, Folklore, Customs, Worship, Festivals, and Superstition, by William Tyler Olcott. ISBN 1-58509-044-1 • 316 pages • 6 x 9 • trade paper • $24.95

Nature Worship: An Account of Phallic Faiths and Practices Ancient and Modern, by the Author of Phallicism with an Introduction by Tedd St. Rain. ISBN 1-58509-049-2 • 112 pages • 6 x 9 • trade paper • illustrated • $12.95

Life and Religion, by Max Muller. ISBN 1-885395-10-8 • 237 pages • 5 1/2 x 8 1/2 • trade paper • $14.95

Jesus: God, Man, or Myth? An Examination of the Evidence, by Herbert Cutner. ISBN 1-58509-072-7 • 304 pages • 6 x 9 • trade paper • $23.95

Pagan and Christian Creeds: Their Origin and Meaning, by Edward Carpenter. ISBN 1-58509-024-7 • 316 pages • 5 1/2 x 8 1/2 • trade paper • $24.95

The Christ Myth: A Study, by Elizabeth Evans. ISBN 1-58509-037-9 • 136 pages • 6 x 9 • trade paper • $13.95

Popery: Foe of the Church and the Republic, by Joseph F. Van Dyke. ISBN 1-58509-058-1 • 336 pages • 6 x 9 • trade paper • illustrated • $25.95

Career of Religious Ideas, by Hudson Tuttle. ISBN 1-58509-066-2 • 172 pages • 5 x 8 • trade paper • $15.95

Buddhist Suttas: Major Scriptural Writings from Early Buddhism, by T.W. Rhys Davids. ISBN 1-58509-079-4 • 376 pages • 6 x 9 • trade paper • $27.95

Early Buddhism, by T. W. Rhys Davids. Includes ***Buddhist Ethics: The Way to Salvation?,*** by Paul Tice. ISBN 1-58509-076-X • 112 pages • 6 x 9 • trade paper • $12.95

The Fountain-Head of Religion: A Comparative Study of the Principal Religions of the World and a Manifestation of their Common Origin from the Vedas, by Ganga Prasad. ISBN 1-58509-054-9 • 276 pages • 6 x 9 • trade paper • $22.95

India: What Can It Teach Us?, by Max Muller. ISBN 1-58509-064-6 • 284 pages • 5 1/2 x 8 1/2 • trade paper • $22.95

Matrix of Power: How the World has Been Controlled by Powerful People Without Your Knowledge, by Jordan Maxwell. ISBN 1-58509-120-0 • 104 pages • 6 x 9 • trade paper • $12.95

Cyberculture Counterconspiracy: A Steamshovel Web Reader, Volume One, edited by Kenn Thomas. ISBN 1-58509-125-1 • 180 pages • 6 x 9 • trade paper • illustrated • $16.95

Cyberculture Counterconspiracy: A Steamshovel Web Reader, Volume Two, edited by Kenn Thomas. ISBN 1-58509-126-X • 132 pages • 6 x 9 • trade paper • illustrated • $13.95

Oklahoma City Bombing: The Suppressed Truth, by Jon Rappoport. ISBN 1-885395-22-1 • 112 pages • 5 1/2 x 8 1/2 • trade paper • $12.95

The Protocols of the Learned Elders of Zion, by Victor Marsden. ISBN 1-58509-015-8 • 312 pages • 6 x 9 • trade paper • $24.95

Secret Societies and Subversive Movements, by Nesta H. Webster. ISBN 1-58509-092-1 • 432 pages • 6 x 9 • trade paper • $29.95

The Secret Doctrine of the Rosicrucians, by Magus Incognito. ISBN 1-58509-091-3 • 256 pages • 6 x 9 • trade paper • $20.95

The Origin and Evolution of Freemasonry: Connected with the Origin and Evolution of the Human Race, by Albert Churchward. ISBN 1-58509-029-8 • 240 pages • 6 x 9 • trade paper • $18.95

The Lost Key: An Explanation and Application of Masonic Symbols, by Prentiss Tucker. ISBN 1-58509-050-6 • 192 pages • 6 x 9 • trade paper • illustrated • $15.95

The Character, Claims, and Practical Workings of Freemasonry, by Rev. C.G. Finney. ISBN 1-58509-094-8 • 288 pages • 6 x 9 • trade paper • $22.95

The Secret World Government or "The Hidden Hand": The Unrevealed in History, by Maj.-Gen., Count Cherep-Spiridovich. ISBN 1-58509-093-X • 270 pages • 6 x 9 • trade paper • $21.95

The Magus, Book One: A Complete System of Occult Philosophy, by Francis Barrett. ISBN 1-58509-031-X • 200 pages • 6 x 9 • trade paper • illustrated • $16.95

The Magus, Book Two: A Complete System of Occult Philosophy, by Francis Barrett. ISBN 1-58509-032-8 • 220 pages • 6 x 9 • trade paper • illustrated • $17.95

The Magus, Book One and Two: A Complete System of Occult Philosophy, by Francis Barrett. ISBN 1-58509-033-6 • 420 pages • 6 x 9 • trade paper • illustrated • $34.90

The Key of Solomon The King, by S. Liddell MacGregor Mathers. ISBN 1-58509-022-0 • 152 pages • 6 x 9 • trade paper • illustrated • $12.95

Magic and Mystery in Tibet, by Alexandra David-Neel. ISBN 1-58509-097-2 • 352 pages • 6 x 9 • trade paper • $26.95

The Comte de St. Germain, by I. Cooper Oakley. ISBN 1-58509-068-9 • 280 pages • 6 x 9 • trade paper • illustrated • $22.95

Alchemy Rediscovered and Restored, by A. Cockren. ISBN 1-58509-028-X • 156 pages • 5 1/2 x 8 1/2 • trade paper • $13.95

The 6th and 7th Books of Moses, with an Introduction by Paul Tice. ISBN 1-58509-045-X • 188 pages • 6 x 9 • trade paper • illustrated • $16.95

www.ingramcontent.com/pod-product-compliance
Lightning Source LLC
Chambersburg PA
CBHW031159270326
41931CB00006B/332